SCHOLASTIC

GRADE 5

Great Math Practice

Previously published as Scholastic Success with Maths by Scholastic

Published by Scholastic India Pvt. Ltd.

A subsidiary of Scholastic Inc., New York, 10012 (USA).

Publishers since 1920, with international operations in Canada, Australia, New Zealand, the United Kingdom, India and Hong Kong.

For information regarding permission, write to:
Scholastic India Pvt. Ltd.
A-27, Ground Floor, Bharti Sigma Centre
Infocity - 1, Sector 34, Gurgaon (Haryana) 122001
Email: education@scholastic.co.in

First edition: 2017

Reprinted: July 2025

ISBN-13: 978-93-5275-291-1

Printed at Shiv Shakti Printing and trading Co., Haryana

Contents

About the Book

"Nothing succeeds like success."
—Alexandre Dumas the Elder, 1854

And no other math resource helps kids succeed like Scholastic Great Math Practice! For classroom or at-home use, this exciting series for kids in grades 1 through 5 provides invaluable reinforcement and practice for math skills such as:

- ❑ number sense and concepts
- ❑ patterns, reasoning and logic
- ❑ basic operations and computations
- ❑ words problems
- ❑ time, money, and measurement
- ❑ fractions and decimals
- ❑ geometry and basic shapes
- ❑ graphs, charts, tables … and more!

Each book contains loads of challenging puzzles, inviting games, and clever practice pages to keep kids delighted and excited as they strengthen their basic math skills.

What makes *Scholastic Great Math Practice* so solid?

- The chapters are aligned to the scope and progression of the NCERT syllabus. This ensures students are engaging with the worksheets in parallel to classroom lessons.
- Each practice page in the series reinforces a specific, age-appropriate skill as outlined by the NCERT.
- These skills give students the ability to interact with the mathematics they see and experience around them, fully meeting the objectives of the NCF.

Take the lead and help kids succeed with *Scholastic Great Math Practice*.
Parents and teachers agree: No one helps kids succeed like Scholastic!

Comparing & Ordering Numbers

Name ______________________ Date __________

Use the digits in the box to answer each number riddle.
You cannot repeat digits within a number.

1 8 3 4 9 6 2 7

1. I am the number that is 100 greater than 3,362.
   What number am I? ______________________

2. I am the number that is 40 less than the largest number you can make using five of the digits.
   What number am I? ______________________

3. I am the largest number you can make that is greater than 8,745 but less than 8,750.
   What number am I? ______________________

4. I am the number that is 5,000 greater than the smallest number you can make using six of the digits.
   What number am I? ______________________

5. I am the smallest number you can make that is greater than 6,17,500.
   What number am I? ______________________

6. I am the largest number you can make that is less than 6,18,400 but greater than 6,18,300.
   What number am I? ______________________

A Stinky Riddle

Name ______________________ Date ____________

Riddle: How do skunks measure length?

Answer each problem. Then, use the Decoder to solve the riddle by filling in the spaces at the bottom of the page.

1. In the number 52,370, the digit 2 is in which place? _______
2. In the number 6,19,246, which digit is in the lakhs place? _______
3. In the number 20,27,635, the digit 3 is in which place? _______
4. In the number 3,71,96,511, which digit is in the ten lakhs place? _______
5. In the number 40,28,19,335, which digit is in the crores place? _______
6. In the number 81,72,48,100, which place is the digit 8 in? _______
7. In the number 54,32,10,789, which place is the digit 4 in? _______
8. Which number is greater: 7,27,912 or 6,99,534? _______
9. Which number is smaller: 48,47,266 or 50,00,122? _______
10. Which number is greater: 44,67,26,012 or 44,67,32,0 _______

Decoder

44,67,26,012....... **K**
ones.................... **P**
1........................ **W**
48,47,266............ **T**
7........................ **N**
thousands............ **I**
6,99,534............. **A**
hundreds............ **O**
4,467,32,011........ **T**
ten crores........... **R**
tens.................... **S**
lakhs.................. **B**
6........................ **E**
50,00,122........... **D**
ten thousands..... **V**
0........................ **E**
crores..................**M**
9........................ **F**
5........................ **H**
7,27,912............. **E**

IN "SC ___ ___ ___" ___ ___ ___ ___ ___ ___ ___

8 4 9 1 7 5 10 6 2 3

Mystery Number

Name ______________________________ Date ______________

Use the digits in the box to answer each number riddle. Digits appear only once in an answer. Each answer may not use all digits.

2 4 9 6 7 3

1. When you subtract a 2-digit number from a 3-digit number, the difference is 473.
   What are the numbers? ______________________

2. The sum of these two numbers is 112.
   What are the numbers? ______________________

3. The sum of these two numbers is 519.
   What are the numbers? ______________________

4. The difference between these two 3-digit numbers is 263.
   What are the numbers? ______________________

5. The sum of these three 2-digit numbers is 184.
   What are the numbers? ______________________

6. The difference between two 3-digit numbers is a palindrome between 200 and 300.
   What are the numbers? ______________________

What Number Am I?

Name ________________________ Date ____________

Use the digits in the box to answer each number riddle.
You cannot repeat digits within a number.

1 2 3 4 5 6 7 8 9

1. I am the largest 4-digit odd number you can make.
   What number am I? ____________________

2. I am the smallest 5-digit even number you can make.
   What number am I? ____________________

3. I am the largest 5-digit even number you can make that has a 3 in the thousands place.
   What number am I? ____________________

4. I am the smallest 5-digit number you can make that has all odd digits.
   What number am I? ____________________

5. I am the largest 6-digit number you can make that has a 1 in the thousands place and a 5 in the ten-thousands place.
   What number am I? ____________________

6. I am the smallest 6-digit even number you can make that has a 6 in the hundreds place.
   What number am I? ____________________

A Place for Every Number

Name ______________________________ Date ______________

Look at the numbers in 243. Each number in the group has its own "place" and meaning. For instance, the 2 in 243 is in the hundreds place. It stands for 2 hundreds or 200. The 4 is in the tens place, meaning 4 tens or 40. And the 3 is in the ones place, meaning 3 ones or 3.

DIRECTIONS:
Use a place value chart to put the numbers in this crossnumber puzzle in their places.

ACROSS

A. 3 hundreds 2 tens 6 ones
C. 8 tens 1 one
E. 6 tens 4 ones
F. 4 tens 7 ones
H. 5 hundreds 2 tens 6 ones
J. 9 tens 3 ones
K. 8 tens 9 ones
M. 5 hundreds 4 tens 2 ones
O. 2 thousands 8 hundreds 3 tens 1 one
Q. 9 tens 8 ones
S. 6 hundreds 6 tens 4 ones

DOWN

A. 3 tens 6 ones
B. 2 thousands 4 hundreds 5 tens 7 ones
D. 1 hundred 4 tens 9 ones
G. 7 tens 3 ones
I. 6 thousands 8 hundreds 5 tens 1 one
L. 9 tens 4 ones
N. 2 hundreds 9 tens 6 ones
P. 3 tens 5
R. 8 tens 4 ones

SUPER CHALLENGE: Make a list of 10 numbers written out in the same way as the clues above. Ask a classmate to write each of those numbers in their own place value box.

Shape Study

Name ______________________________ Date ______________

A heptagon has 7 sides. In a heptagon, all the sides are the same length.

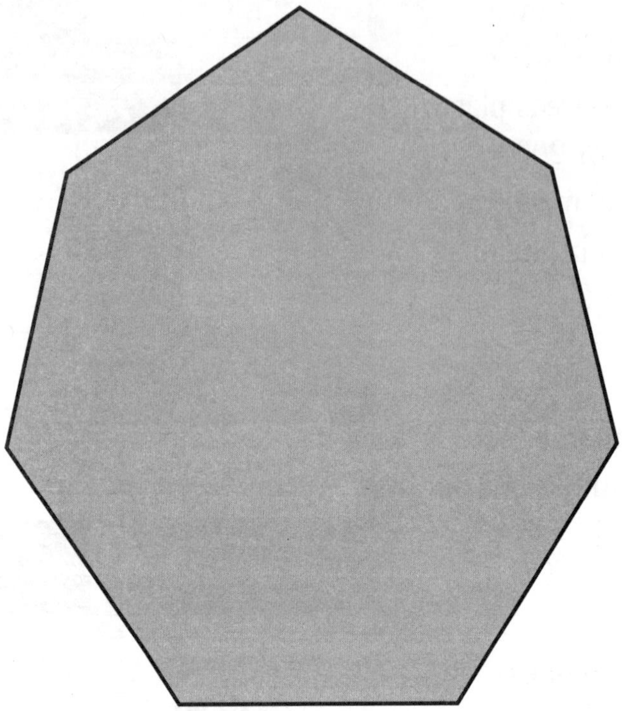

Connect the dots in the geoboards below to make other shapes with 7 sides.

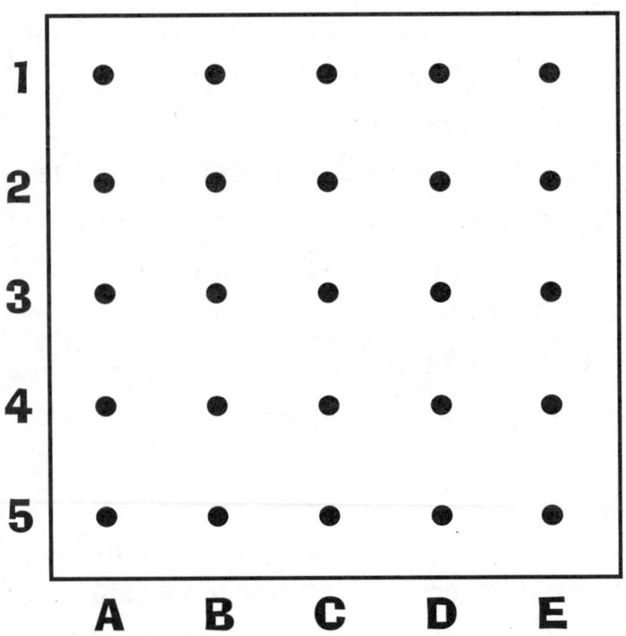

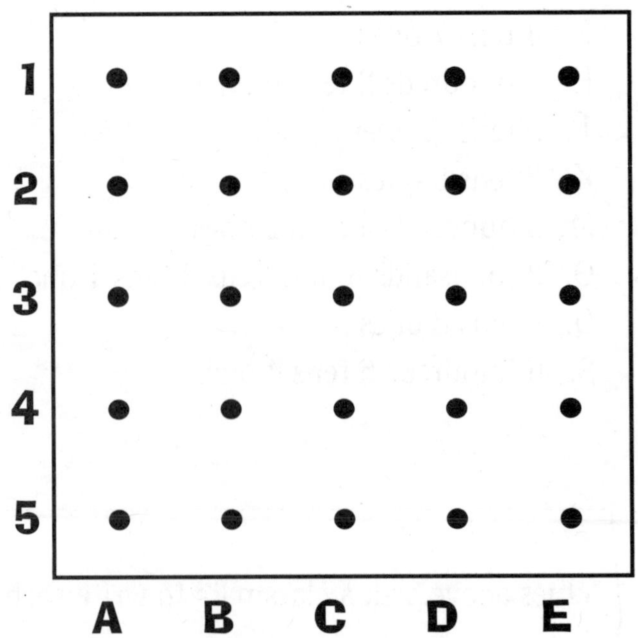

Angles from A to Z

Name ______________________________ Date ______________

Angles are hiding everywhere—even in the words you're reading now. When two straight lines meet, they make an angle. There are three kinds of angles:

- The corner of a square or rectangle makes a right angle.
- Angles that are smaller than right angles are called acute angles.
- Angles that are larger than right angles are called obtuse angles.

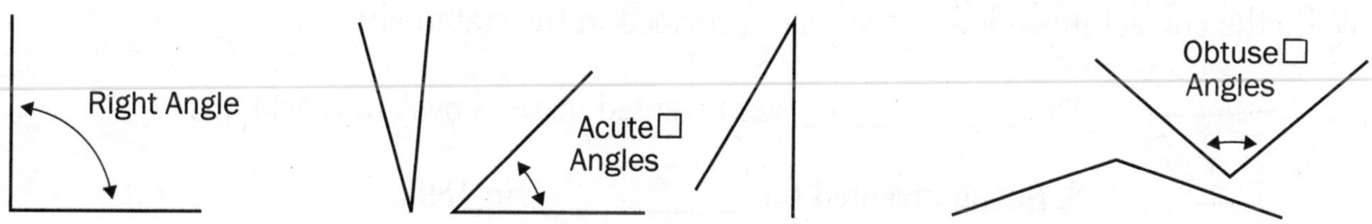

Take a look at the letters below. Circle each angle you see in the letters. Tell whether it is right, acute, or obtuse.

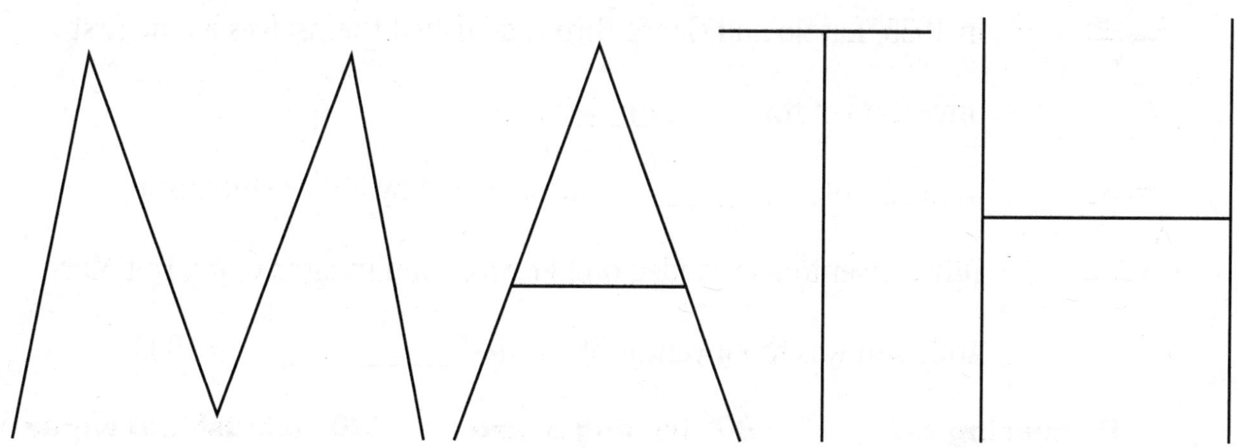

Get an "Angle" on Inventions

Name ______________________________ Date ______________

✏ Everything that people use in their daily lives was invented by someone—things like the ironing board, the cash register, and ear muffs. In this activity, we ask you to match inventions such as these to their inventor. Follow the directions below to get a new "angle" on a few famous inventions.

40° 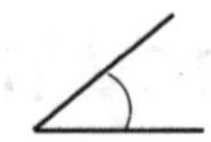

90° 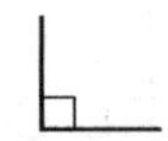

180° 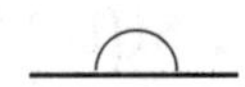

DIRECTIONS:

- Take a look at the angle that appears before each statement.
- Estimate the measure of the angle in degrees using the 40°, 90°, and 180° angles as a guide.
- Next, circle the name of the invention that appears next to the best estimate of that angle.
- Write the correct invention in the space provided in the statement.

1.  The ____________ was invented in 1888 by A.B. Blackburn.
2. 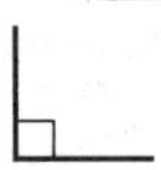 S. Boone invented the ____________ in 1892.
3. 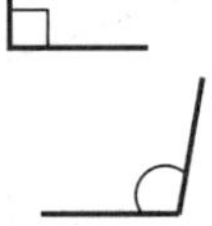 The ____________ was invented in 1912 by Garrett A. Morgan.
4.  The ____________ was invented in 1879 by James Ritty.
5. 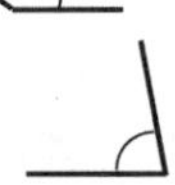 In 1877, Chester Greenwood invented ____________.
6.  In 1935, Laszlo and Georg Biro established themselves as the first inventors of the ____________.
7. In 1902, the ____________ was invented by Miller Hutchison.
8.  Other inventors expanded on her invention in later years. But Mary Anderson was the inventor of the first ____________ in 1903.

11° hearing aid **90° ironing board** **130° windshield wiper**

160° cash register **80° ear muffs** **175° railway signal**

20° ballpoint pen **110° gas mask**

Angles Study

Name ______________________________ Date ______________

Tell if each angle is
less than 90°,
exactly 90° (a right angle),
greater than 90°, or
180°.

1.

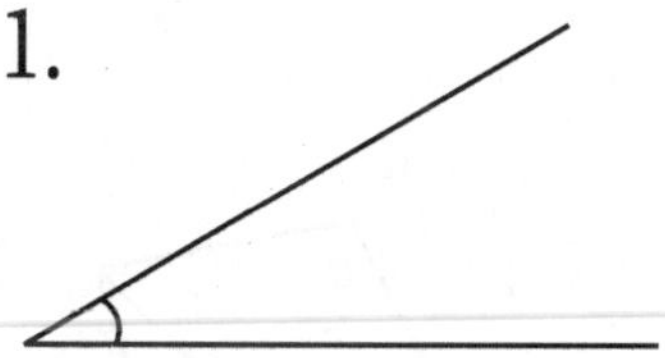

2.

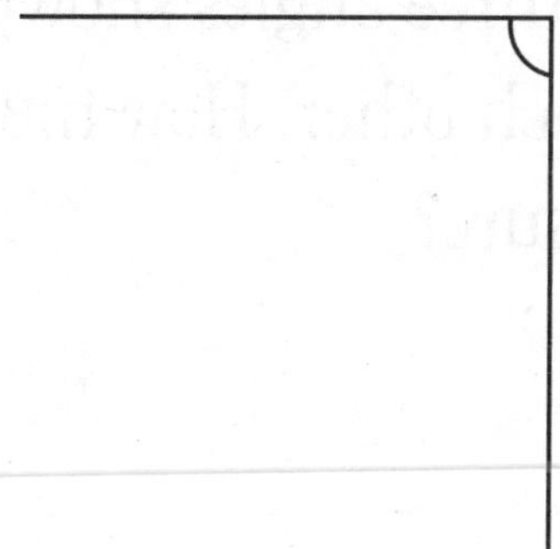

3.

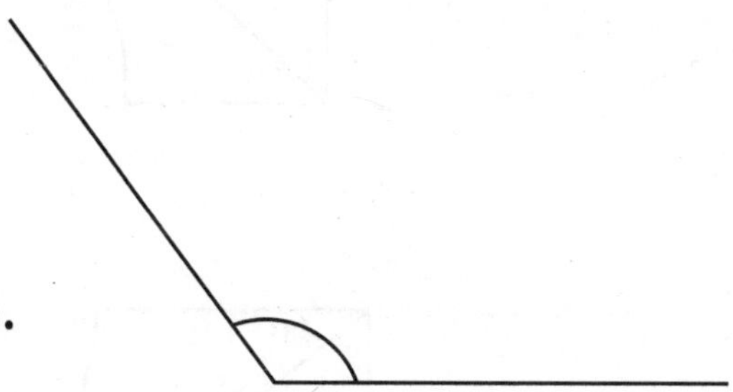

4.

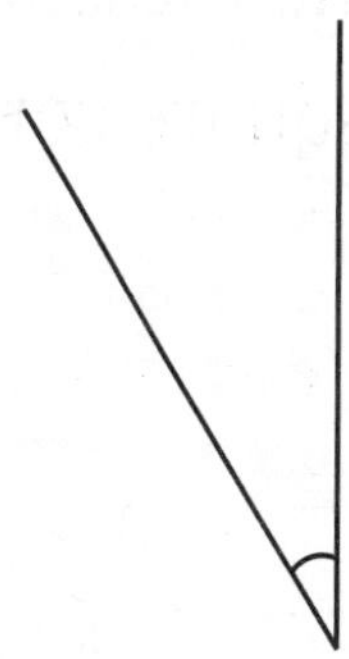

5.

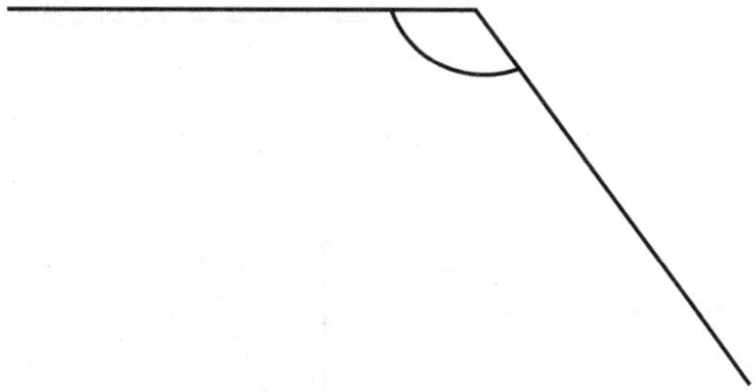

6.

7.

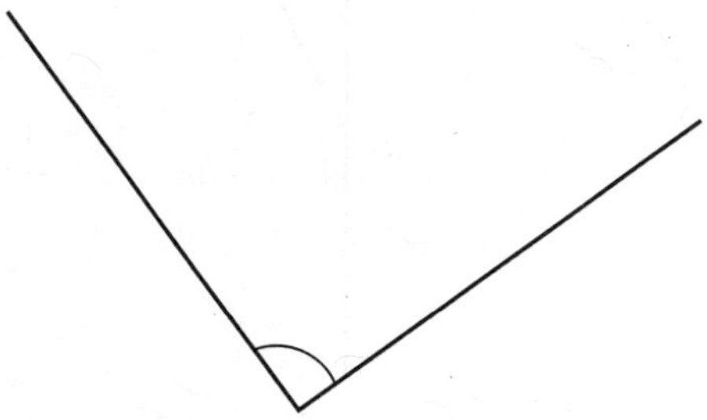

8.

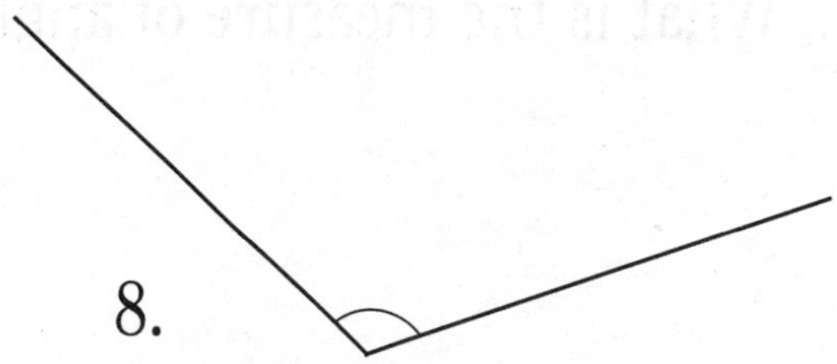

It All Adds Up

Name ______________________________ Date ______________

1. This is a square drawn on a straight line. What is the measure of angle a?

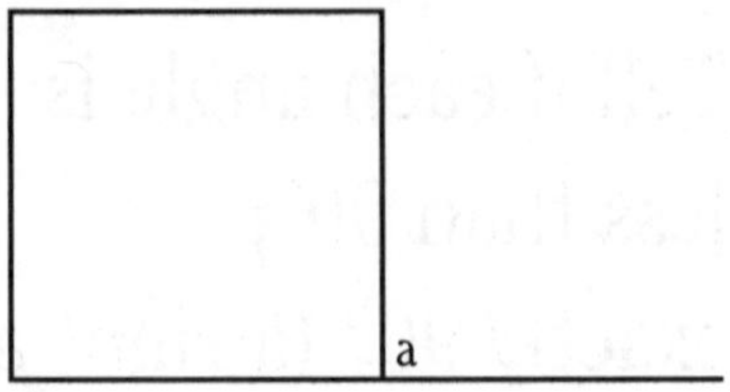

2. The three angles shown are equal to each other. How much does each measure?

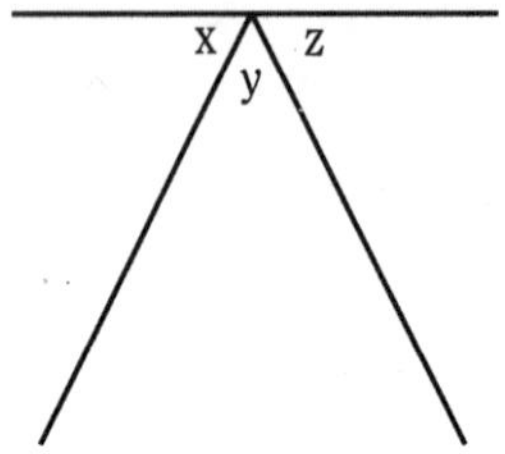

3. What is the measure of angle x, that makes a square corner with the 70° angle?

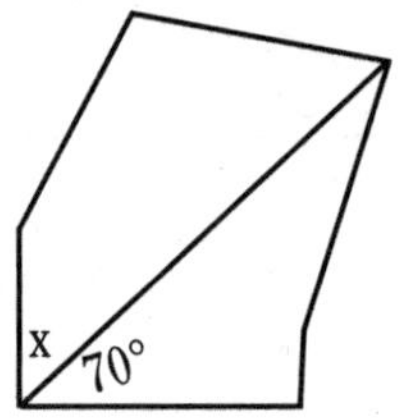

4. In this square corner, find angle y.

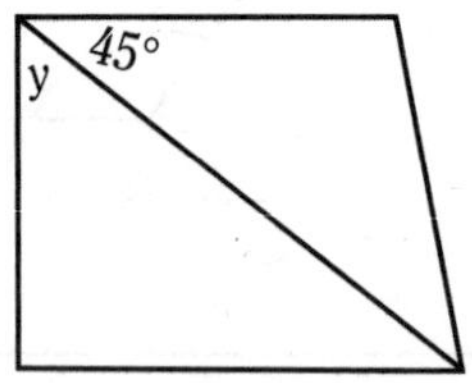

5. What is the measure of angle q?

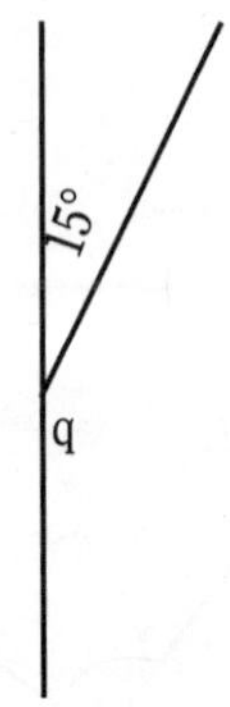

Counting Squares

Name ______________________________ Date ______________

Write the area of the shaded portion. In each set, tell which one has the least area.

1.

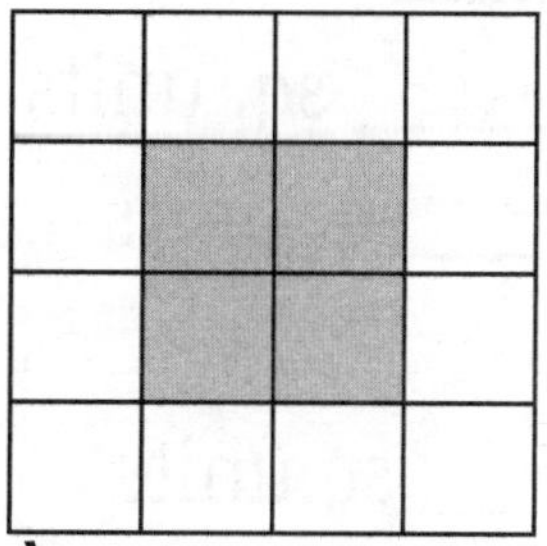

A. _______ sq. units

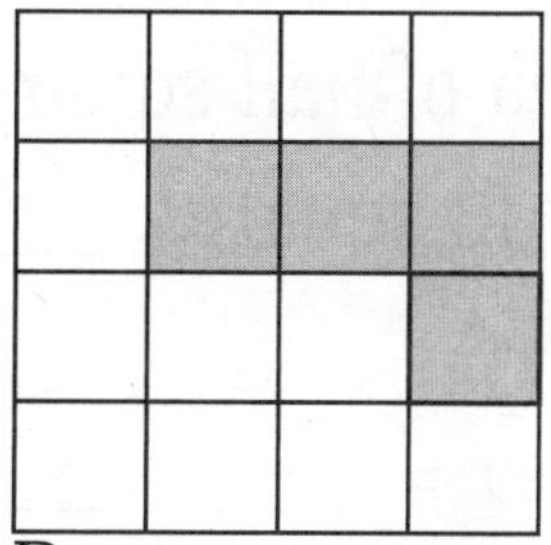

B. _______ sq. units

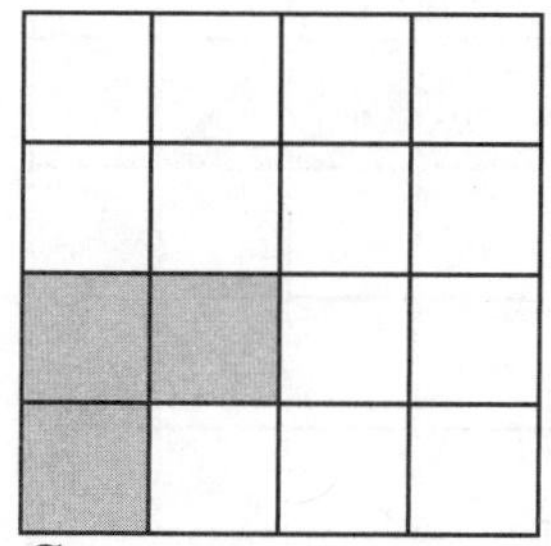

C._______ sq. units

2.

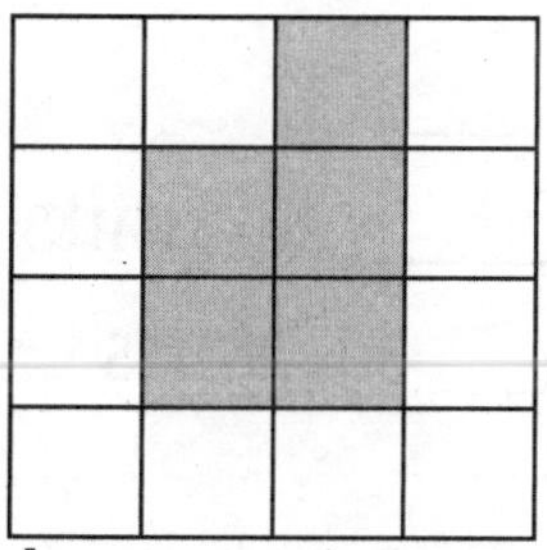

A. _______ sq. units

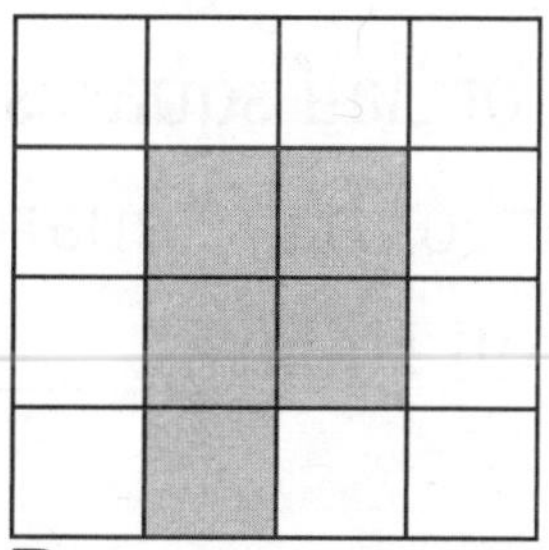

B. _______ sq. units

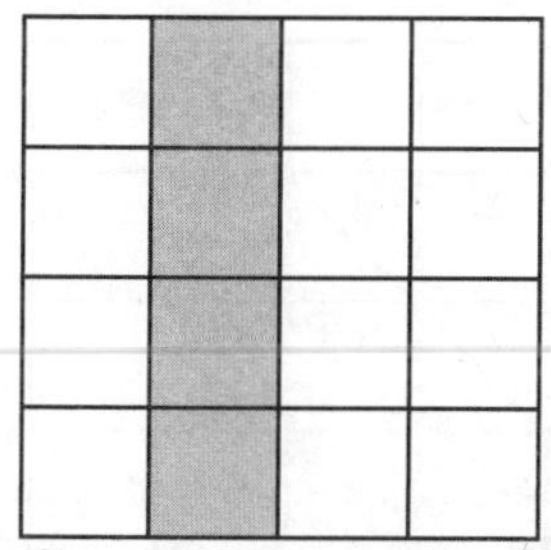

C._______ sq. units

3.

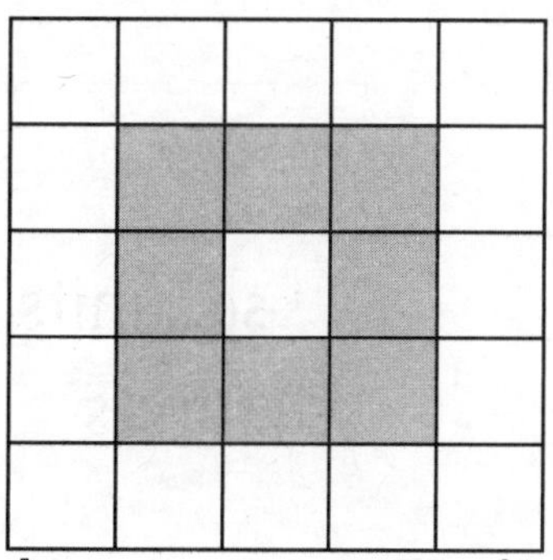

A. _______ sq. units

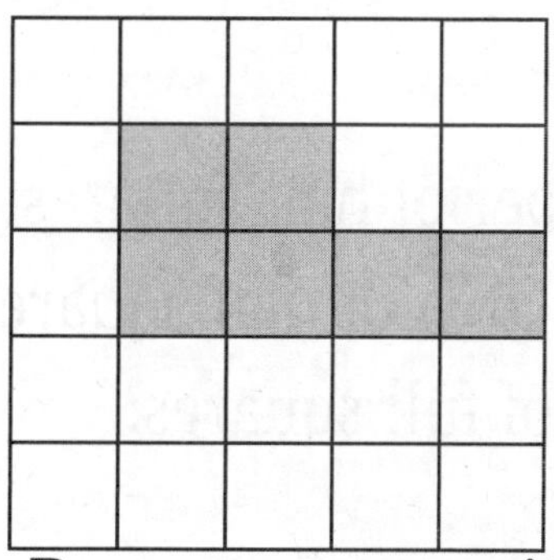

B. _______ sq. units

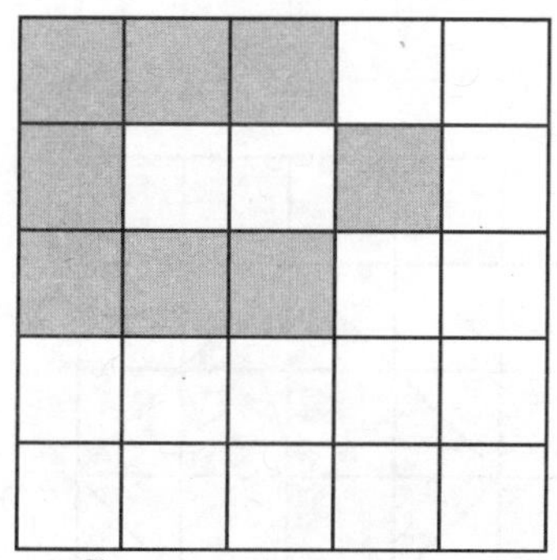

C._______ sq. units

4.

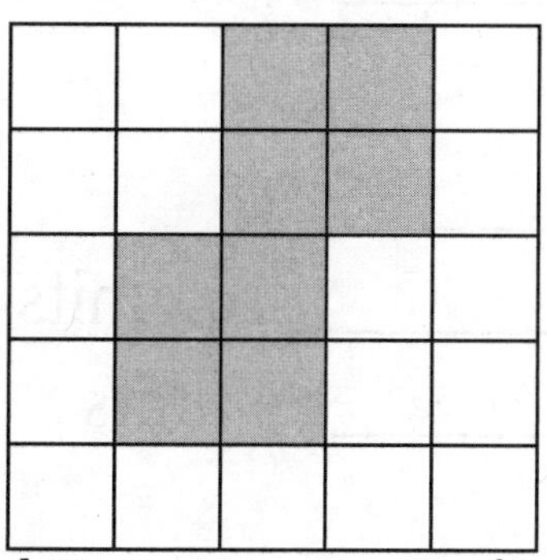

A. _______ sq. units

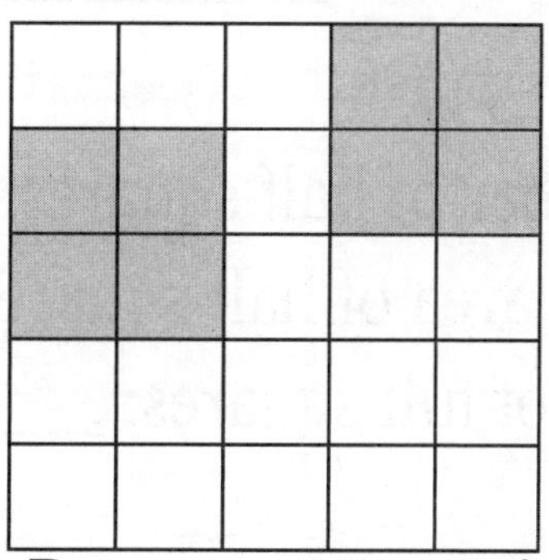

B. _______ sq. units

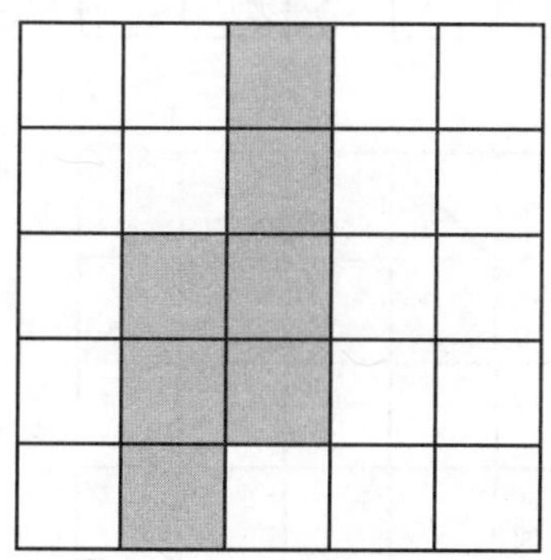

C._______ sq. units

Counting and Adding

Name ______________________________ Date ____________

Examine the shaded area and answer the questions:

1. 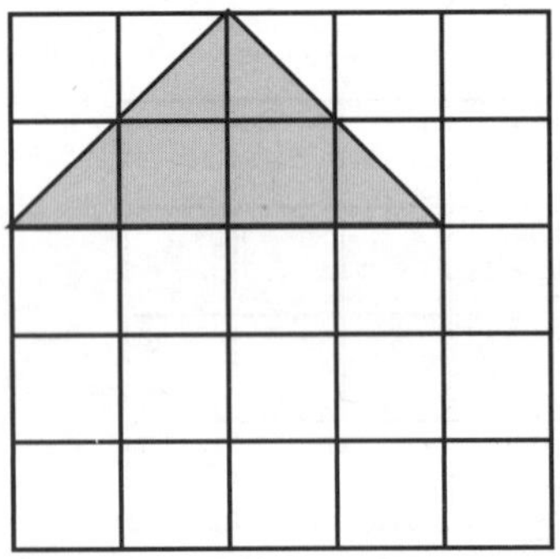

Number of half squares: __________

Total area of half squares: __________ sq. units

Area of full squares: ____________ sq. units

Total area = __________________ sq.units

2. 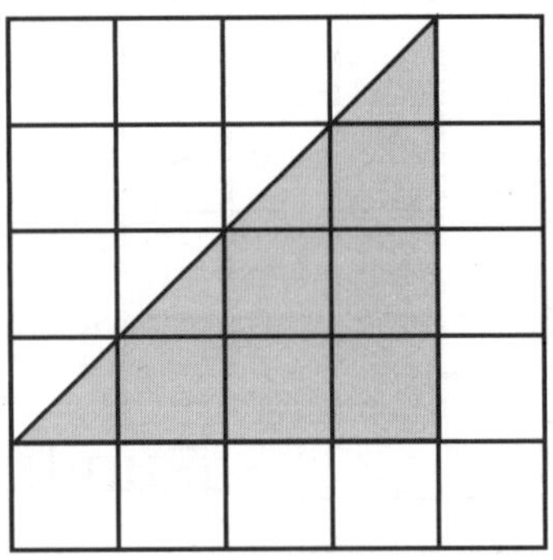

Number of half squares: __________

Total area of half squares: __________ sq. units

Area of full squares: ____________ sq. units

Total area = __________________ sq.units

3. 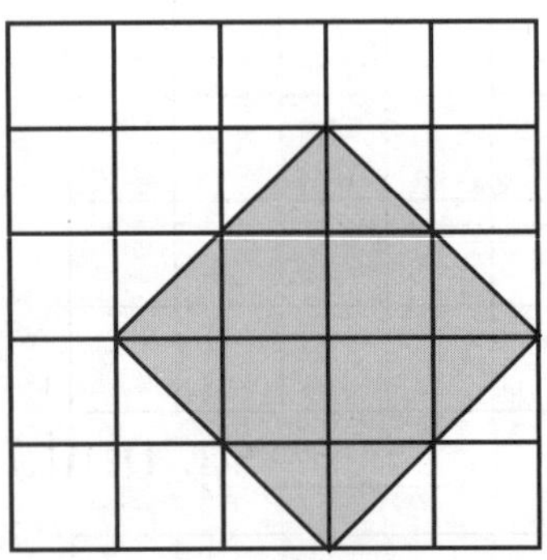

Number of half squares: __________

Total area of half squares: __________ sq. units

Area of full squares: ____________ sq. units

Total area = __________________ sq.units

4. 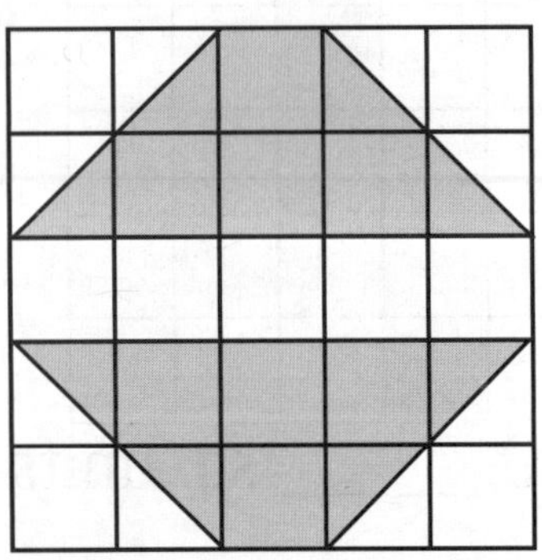

Number of half squares: __________

Total area of half squares: __________ sq. units

Area of full squares: ____________ sq. units

Total area = __________________ sq.units

Cover or Close?

Name ______________________________ Date ______________

In order to find....	....I will use (tick one) AREA	Perimeter
1. The amount of lace I need to put on the edge of a table-cloth	☐	☐
2. The number of tiles of size 1 m × 1 m I need to cover my kitchen floor	☐	☐
3. The amount of barbed-wire I need to fence off my entire garden	☐	☐
4. The amount of rope I need to lay around the boundary of the cricket field	☐	☐
5. The amount of carpet I need to cover the library floor	☐	☐
6. The amount of ribbon I need to put around the rim of the party-hats	☐	☐

Around We Go

Name ______________________________ Date ______________

Draw rough free-hand 4-sided figures with the perimeter indicated below, mentioning the lengths of the sides. The first one has been done for you.

1. Perimeter = 18 units

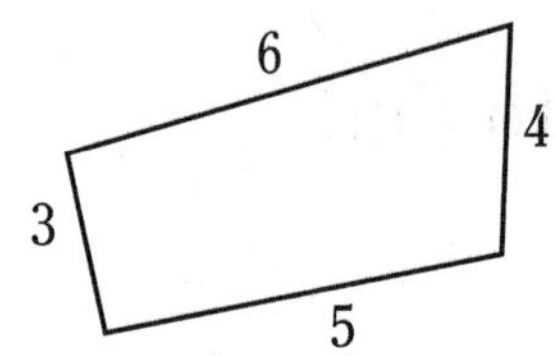

2. Perimeter = 20 units

3. Perimeter = 12 units

4. Perimeter = 24 units

5. Perimeter = 50 units

More Parts to Colour

Name ______________________________ Date ______________

A fraction has two numbers. The top number will tell you how many parts to colour. The bottom number tells you how many parts there are.

a) Colour 1/8 of the circle.

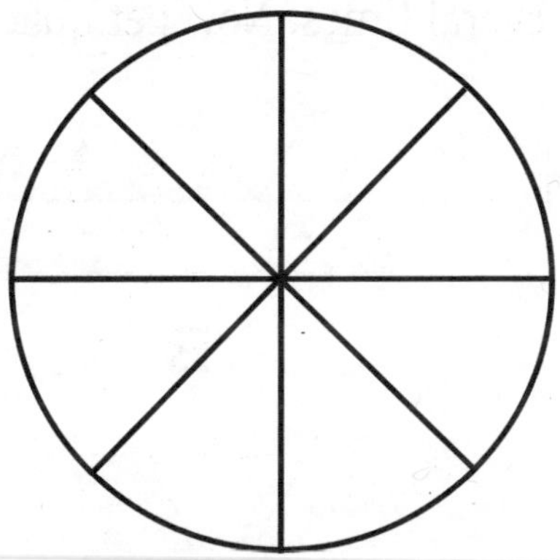

b) Colour 6/8 of the rectangle.

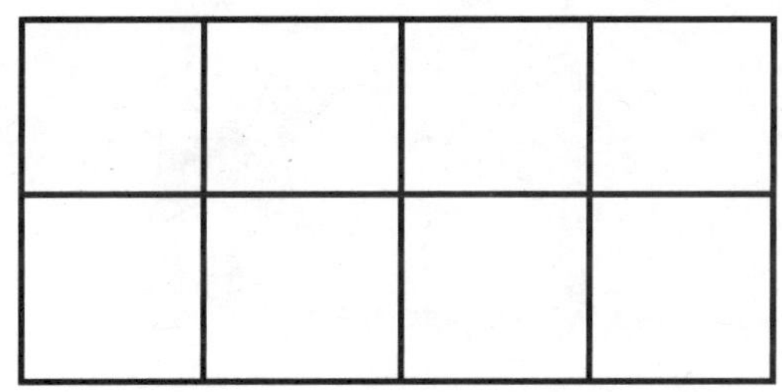

c) Colour 4/8 of the suns.

d) Colour 8/8 of the stars.

e) Colour 2/8 of the moons.

f) Colour 3/8 of the planets.

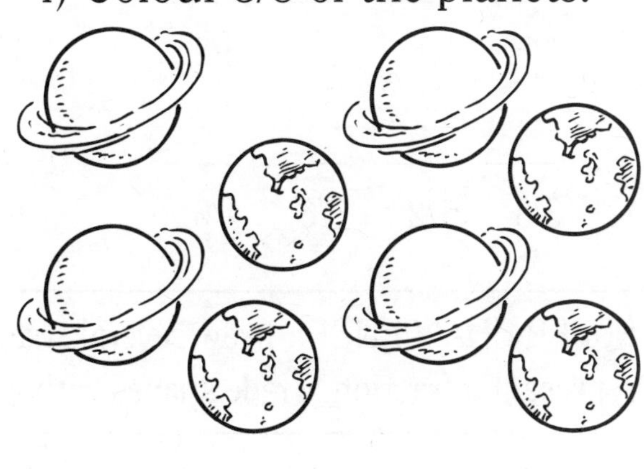

Duck Into Action With Fractions

Name ______________________________ Date ______________

Why don't ducks like to get mail? Fractions can help you find the answer. Each of the shapes below represent a fraction and a letter. To figure out each fraction, compare the number of shaded spaces in the shape to the total number of spaces.

Example: 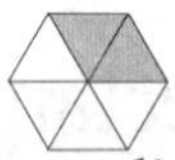 is the same as 2/6. Next, write the letter that is underneath each shape on the corresponding blank below. You will use some letters several times. Now get quacking!

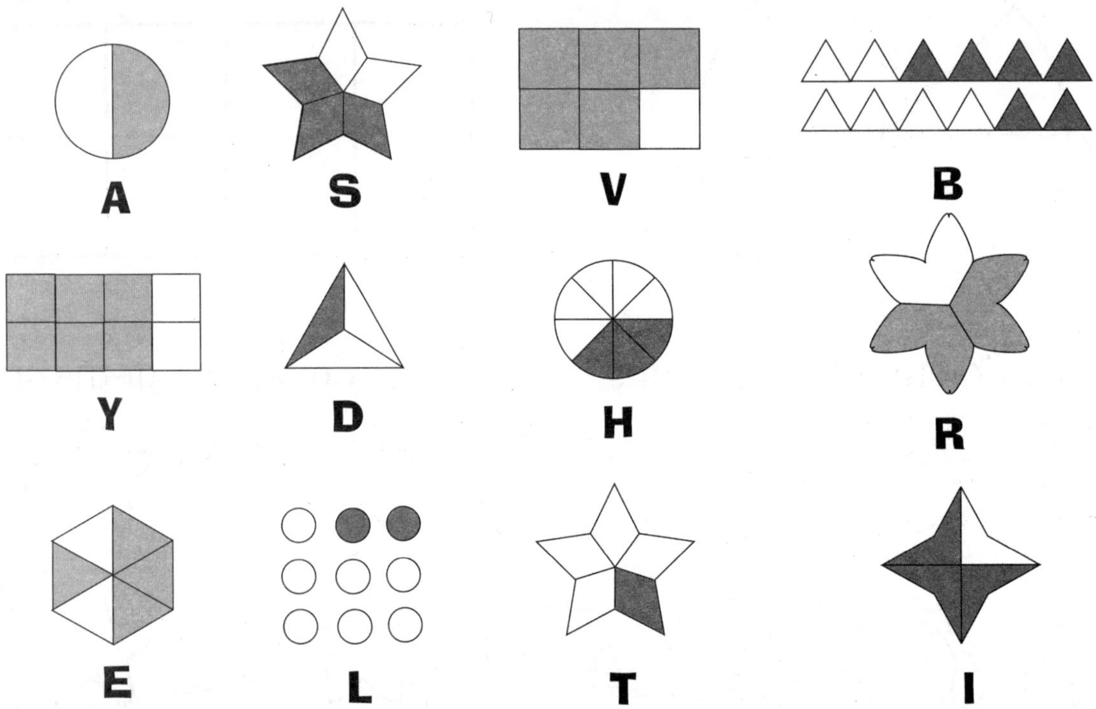

Why don't ducks like to get mail?

___	___	___	___		___	___	___	___	___	___	___
1/5	3/8	4/6	6/8		1/2	2/9	2/3	4/6	1/2	1/3	6/8

___	___	___	___		___	___	___	___	___.
3/8	1/2	5/6	4/6		6/12	3/4	2/9	2/9	3/5

SUPER CHALLENGE: Draw several shapes of your own. Shade in parts of the shape to represent a fraction. Trade shapes with a classmate and identify the fractions shown.

Part Timer

Name ______________________________ Date ______________

Determine fractions of a whole. Check √ your answers.

1. HOW MUCH JUICE IS LEFT?

$\frac{1}{2}$ $\frac{1}{4}$ $\frac{1}{3}$

2. HOW MUCH PIZZA IS GONE?

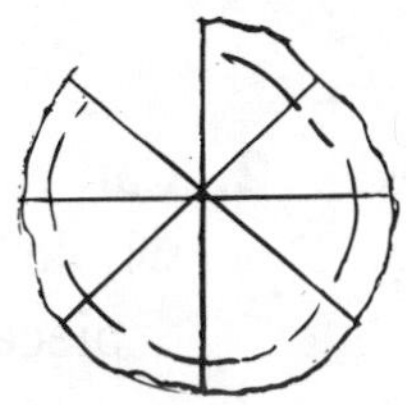

$\frac{1}{2}$ $\frac{1}{3}$ $\frac{1}{8}$

3. HOW MUCH HAS BEEN EATEN?

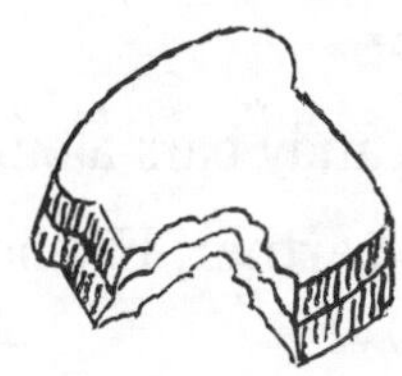

$\frac{1}{3}$ $\frac{1}{6}$ $\frac{1}{4}$

4. HOW MUCH IS GONE?

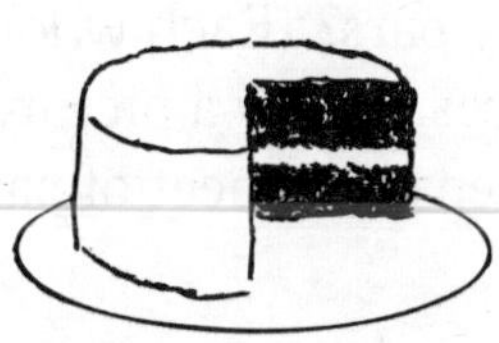

$\frac{1}{4}$ $\frac{1}{2}$ $\frac{1}{6}$

5. HOW MUCH IS LACED?

$\frac{1}{2}$ $\frac{1}{3}$ $\frac{1}{4}$

6. HOW MUCH WATER IS LEFT?

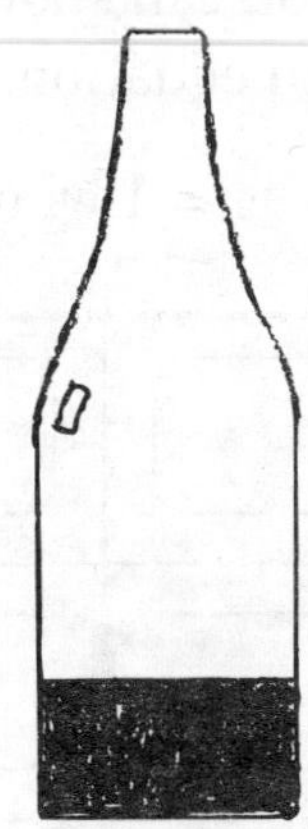

$\frac{1}{6}$ $\frac{1}{4}$ $\frac{1}{3}$

7. HOW MUCH WATER IS LEFT?

$\frac{3}{4}$ $\frac{1}{2}$ $\frac{1}{4}$

8. HOW MUCH HAS BEEN CUT OFF?

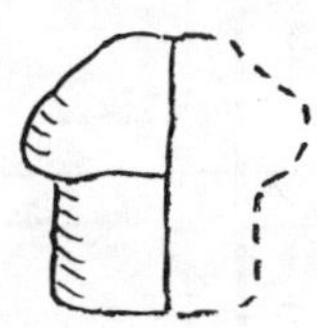

$\frac{1}{2}$ $\frac{1}{3}$ $\frac{1}{4}$

9. HOW MUCH WATER REMAINS?

$\frac{3}{4}$ $\frac{1}{2}$ $\frac{1}{4}$

10. HOW MUCH LEAF HAS BEEN EATEN?

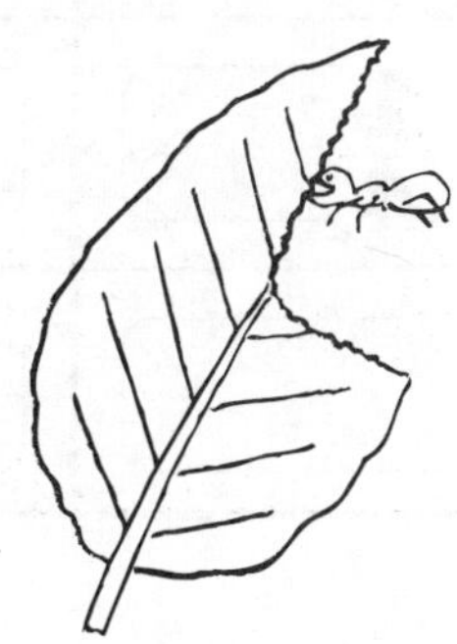

$\frac{1}{4}$ $\frac{1}{6}$ $\frac{2}{3}$

11. HOW MUCH BREAD IS UNCUT?

$\frac{1}{4}$ $\frac{1}{3}$ $\frac{1}{2}$

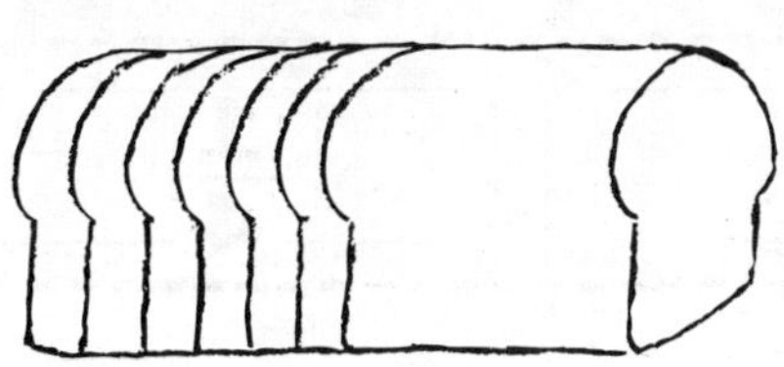

Handy Dandy Fraction Candy

Name ______________________________ Date ______________

Use these candy bars to see just how sweet fractions can be!

You Need:
scissors

What to Do:

- Cut out the candy bars along the dashed lines.
- Work with a partner. Use both candy bars to do the activity.

1. Arrange some of the pieces this way to make a whole bar:

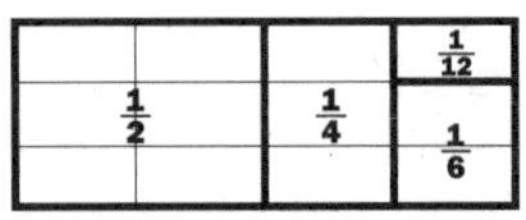

Here's how you can show that combination of fractions in an equation:

$\frac{1}{2} + \frac{1}{4} + \frac{1}{6} + \frac{1}{12} = 1$ whole candy bar

2. Can you find another way to make one whole candy bar without using the $\frac{1}{2}$ piece? What would it look like? How would you write it in a fraction equation?

3. How many ways can you use the pieces to make whole candy bars? (Each whole bar will have 12 pieces.) Draw a picture of each solution on a separate sheet of paper.

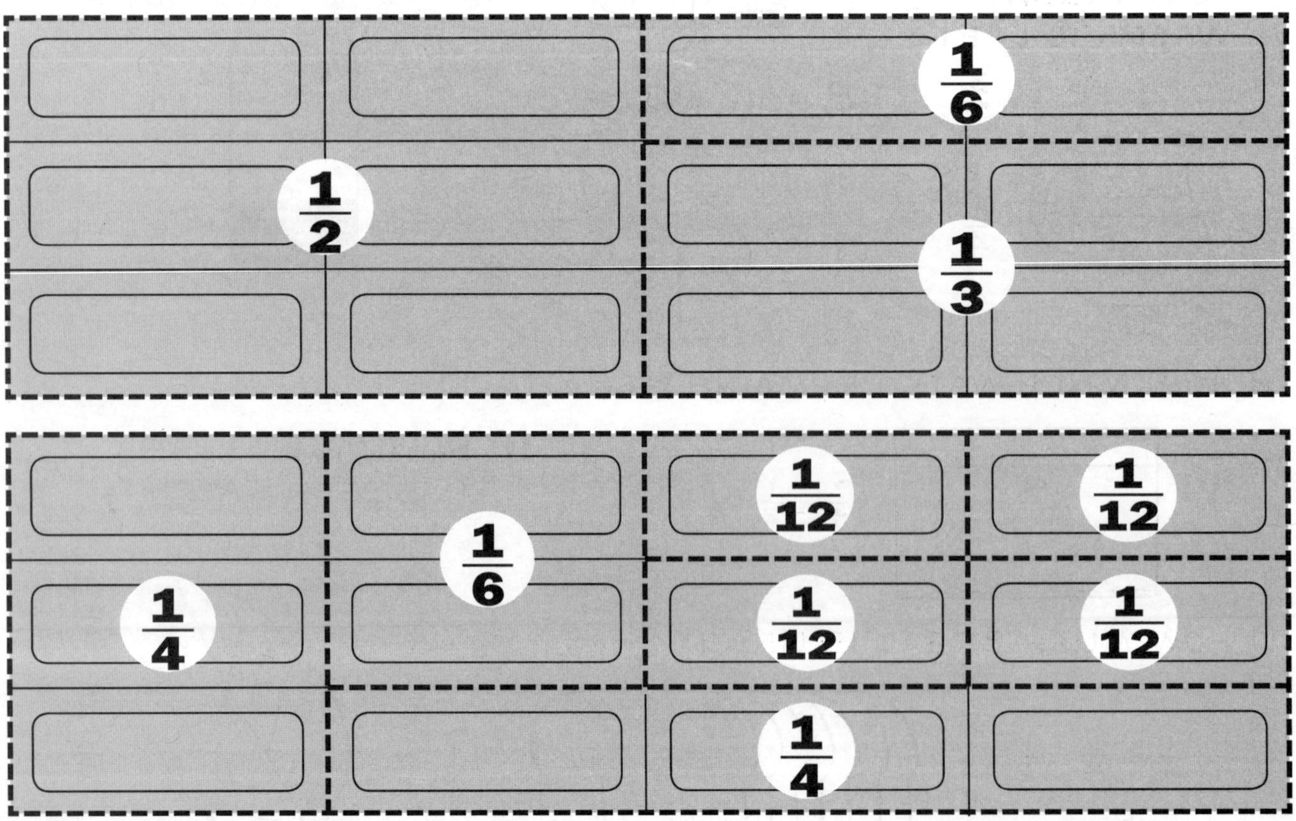

Flag Wagger

Name ______________________________ Date ______________

Write a fraction for the section of the flag next to the arrow.

1. PANAMA

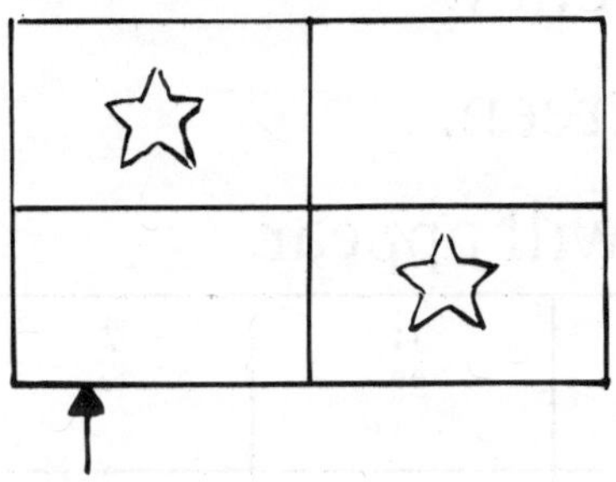

______

2. NIGERIA

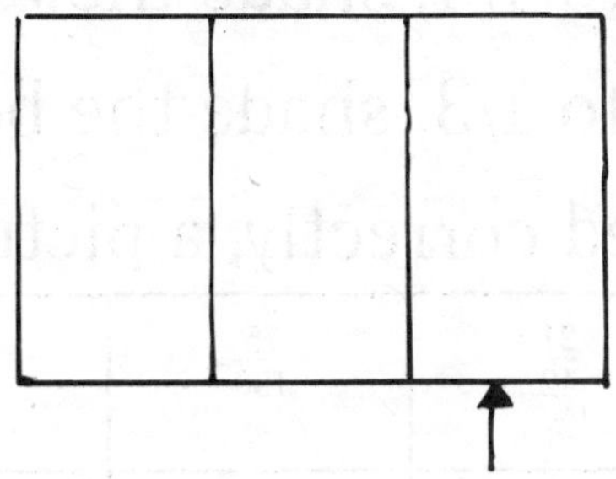

______

3. MADAGASCAR

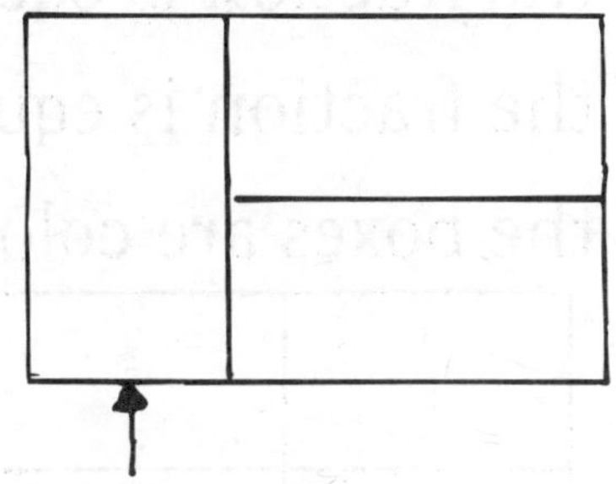

______

4. MALTA

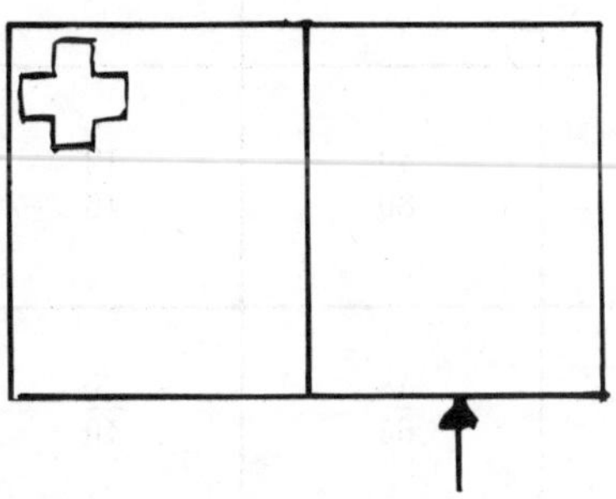

______

5. POLAND

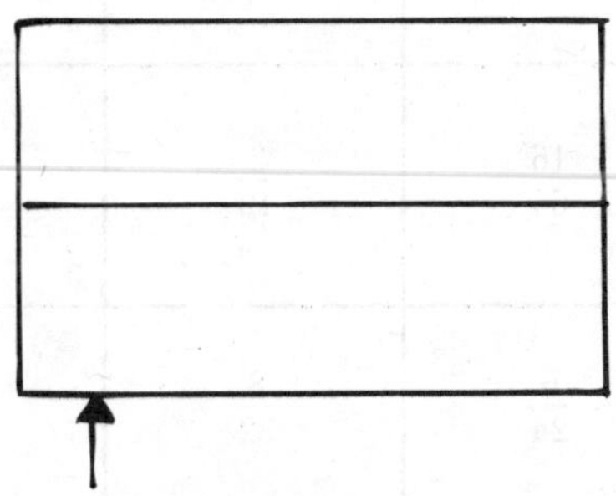

______

6. MAURITIUS

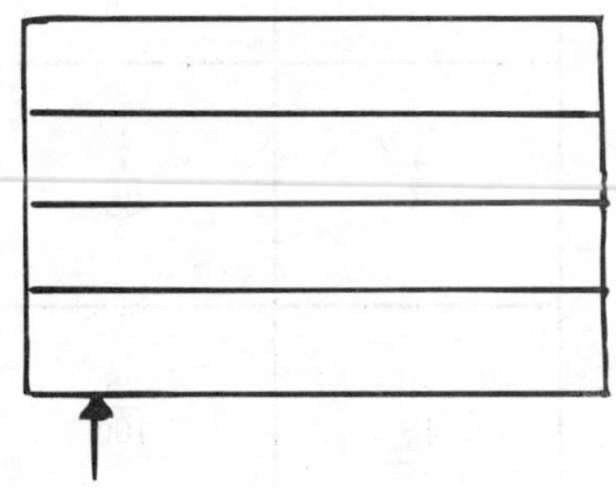

______

7. RUSSIA

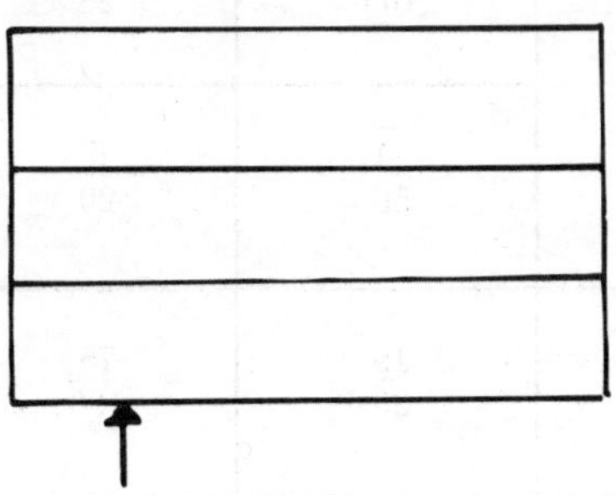

______

8. CHILE

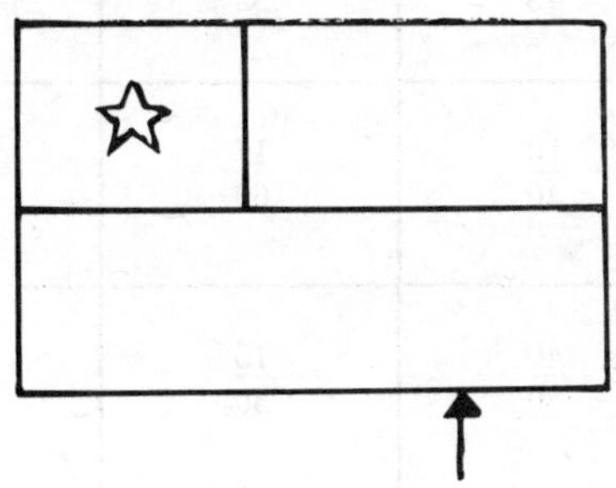

______

9. CZECH REPUBLIC

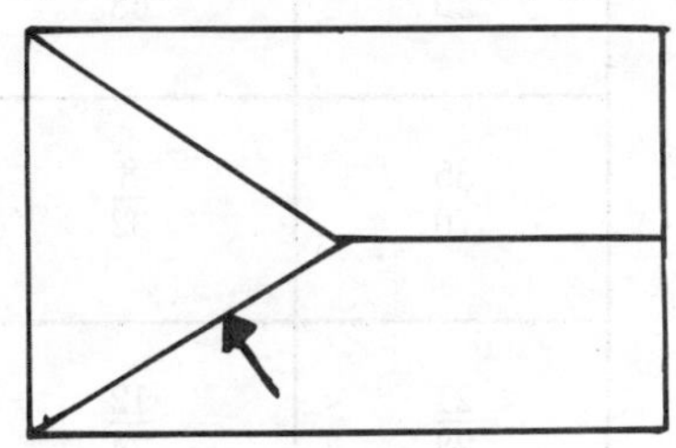

______

10. TAIWAN

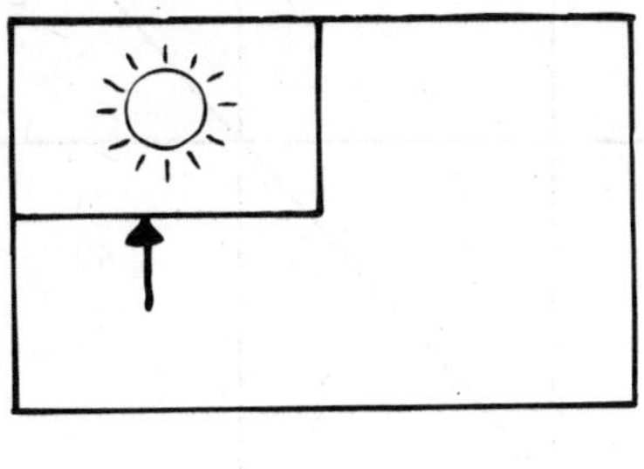

______

11. UNITED ARAB EMIRATES

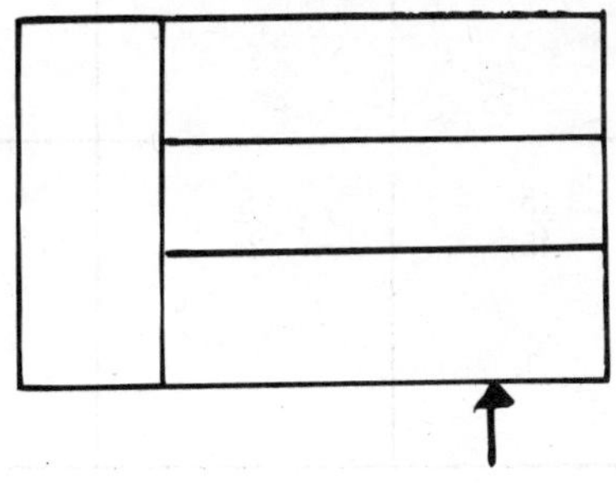

______

12. MALAWI

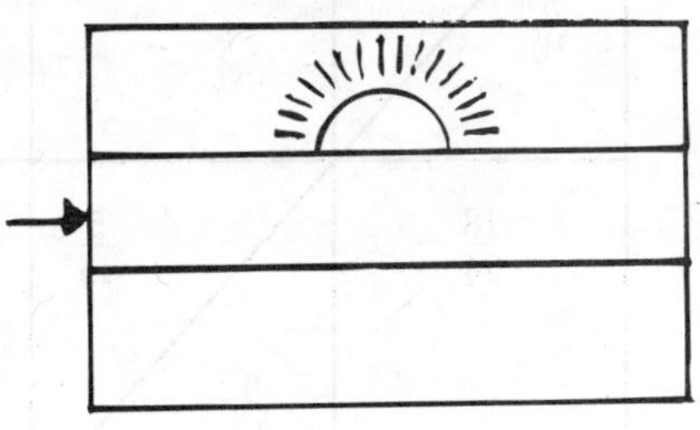

______

Fractions Are a Breeze

Name ______________________________ Date ______________

Sail into fractions by renaming each fraction below in lowest terms.

If the fraction is equal to 1/2 or 3/4, shade the box blue.

If the fraction is equal to 1/4, shade the box yellow.

If the fraction is equal to 1/3, shade the box green.

If the boxes are coloured correctly, a picture will appear.

$\frac{3}{6}$	$\frac{2}{8}$	$\frac{21}{42}$	$\frac{75}{150}$	$\frac{31}{62}$	$\frac{11}{22}$	$\frac{7}{14}$
$\frac{50}{100}$	$\frac{9}{36}$	$\frac{11}{44}$	$\frac{32}{64}$	$\frac{30}{60}$	$\frac{6}{12}$	$\frac{60}{120}$
$\frac{4}{8}$	$\frac{7}{28}$	$\frac{16}{64}$	$\frac{3}{12}$	$\frac{8}{16}$	$\frac{40}{80}$	$\frac{12}{16}$
$\frac{9}{18}$	$\frac{25}{100}$	$\frac{6}{24}$	$\frac{8}{32}$	$\frac{19}{76}$	$\frac{48}{64}$	$\frac{5}{10}$
$\frac{10}{20}$	$\frac{17}{68}$	$\frac{12}{48}$	$\frac{13}{52}$	$\frac{20}{80}$	$\frac{25}{100}$	$\frac{14}{28}$
$\frac{35}{70}$	$\frac{8}{32}$	$\frac{10}{40}$	$\frac{15}{60}$	$\frac{40}{160}$	$\frac{14}{56}$	$\frac{5}{20}$
$\frac{21}{28}$	$\frac{12}{24}$	$\frac{40}{80}$	$\frac{15}{30}$	$\frac{33}{66}$	$\frac{15}{20}$	$\frac{75}{100}$
$\frac{2}{6}$ / $\frac{5}{10}$	$\frac{12}{36}$	$\frac{9}{27}$	$\frac{30}{90}$	$\frac{20}{60}$	$\frac{11}{33}$	$\frac{6}{18}$ / $\frac{2}{4}$
$\frac{18}{24}$	$\frac{5}{15}$ / $\frac{9}{12}$	$\frac{15}{45}$	$\frac{8}{24}$	$\frac{10}{30}$	$\frac{3}{9}$ / $\frac{6}{8}$	$\frac{30}{40}$

Bon Voyage!

Shape Study

Name ______________________________ Date ______________

"Symmetry" exists when the two halves of something are mirror images of each other. Look at the pictures below. Color those that show symmetry. (Hint: Imagine the pictures are folded on the dotted lines.)

Complete the drawings below. Connect the dots to show the other half. (Hint: The pictures are symmetrical!)

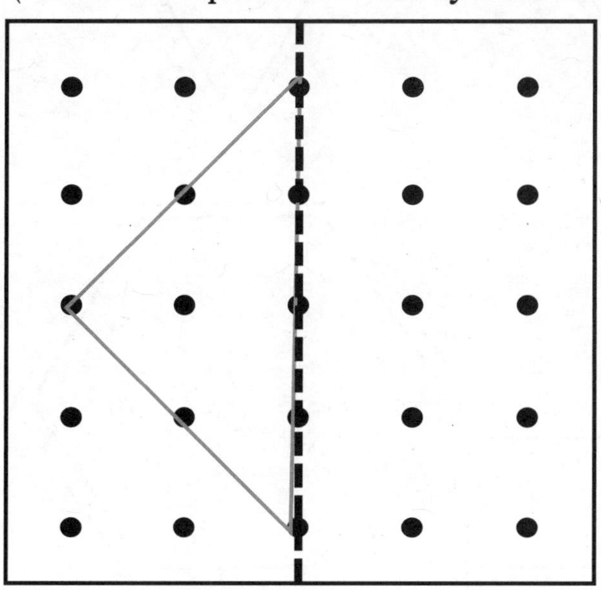

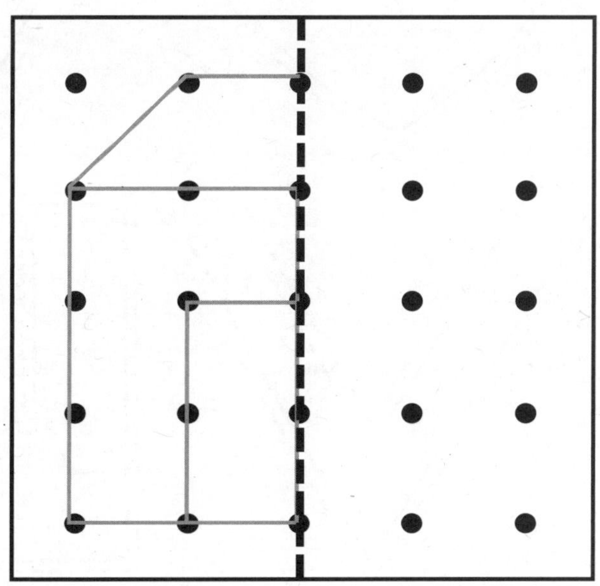

Shape Symmetry

Name ______________________ Date ____________

Janis folded all her shapes in half. Some were symmetrical—one half matched the other half. Some shapes were not symmetrical.

1. Try and fold these shapes in half by making a crease that runs from top to bottom. Which ones are symmetrical?

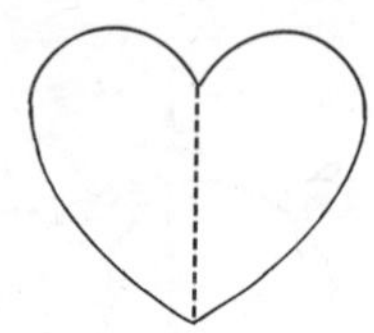

_______________ _______________

_______________ _______________

2. If you could fold the shapes by making a crease running from left to right, which shapes would be symmetrical this way? ______________

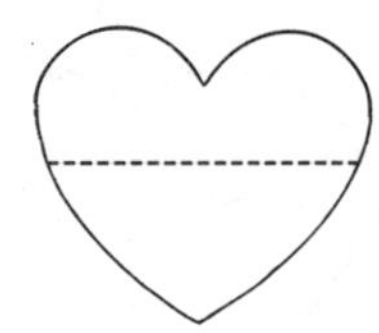

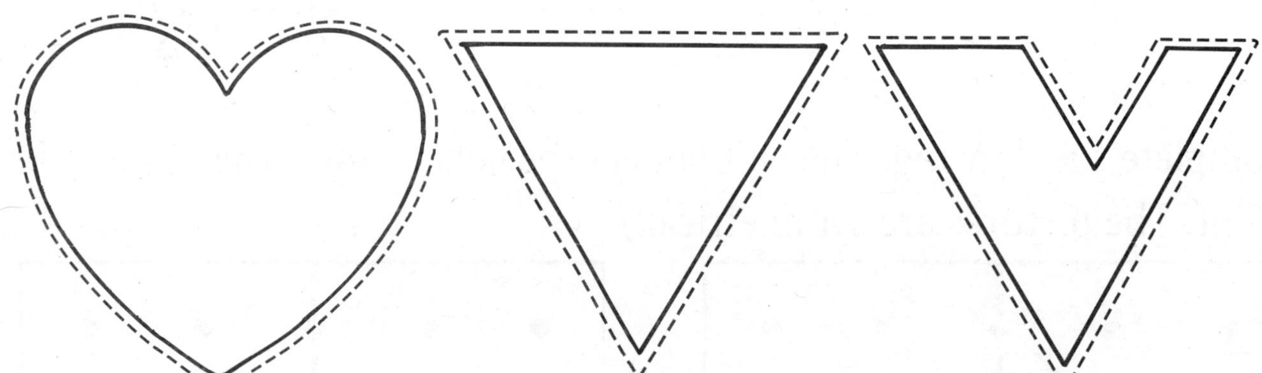

A. B. C.

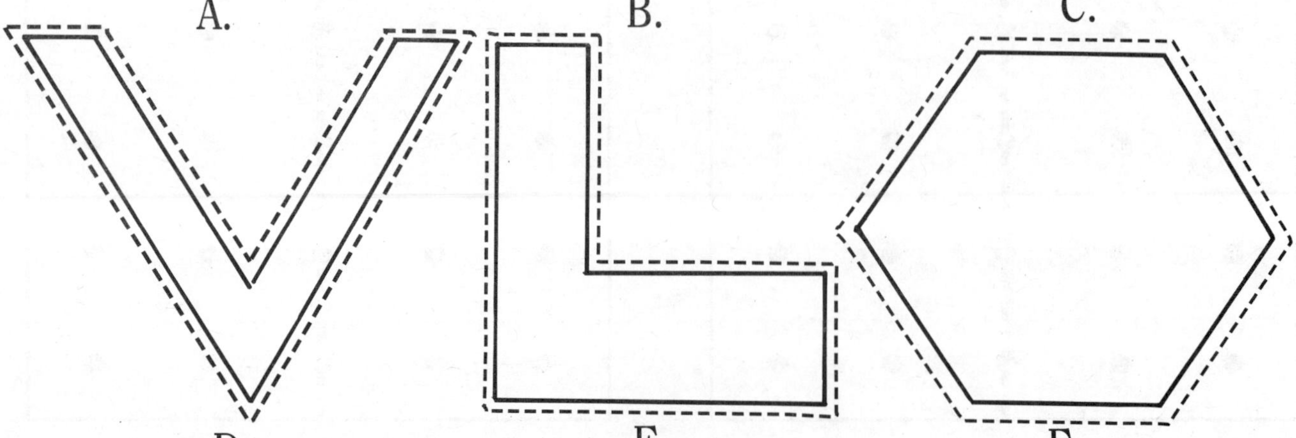

D. E. F.

Mirror Half

Name ______________________________ Date ______________

Draw the missing half of each shape.

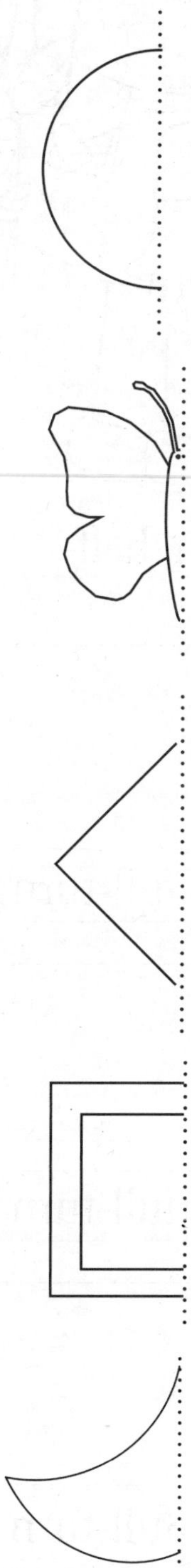

Spinning around

Name ______________________________ Date ______________

Look at this shape. 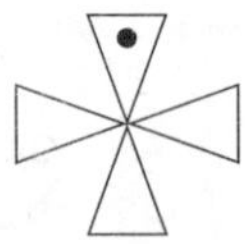

This is what it would look like after ....

...a quarter-turn 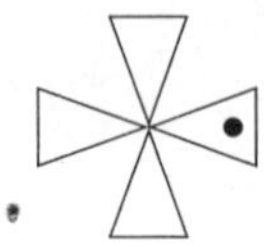

...a half-turn 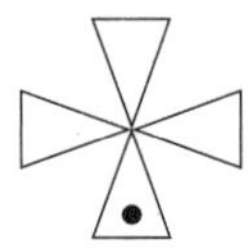

...a full-turn 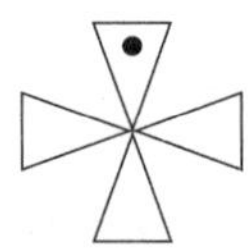

Draw what these shapes would look like after a quarter-turn, half-turn, a full-turn from the original position.

quarter-turn	half-turn	full-turn

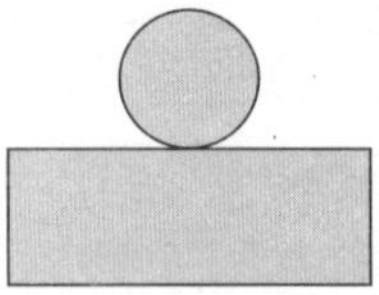

quarter-turn	half-turn	full-turn

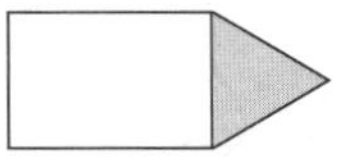

quarter-turn	half-turn	full-turn

Branching Out

Name ______________________________ Date ______________

Complete these factor-trees.

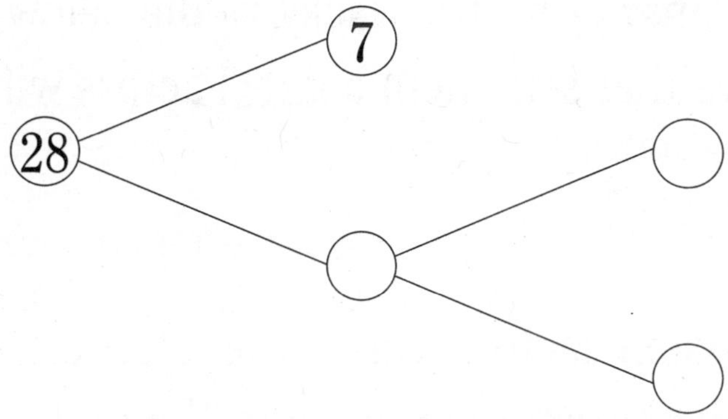

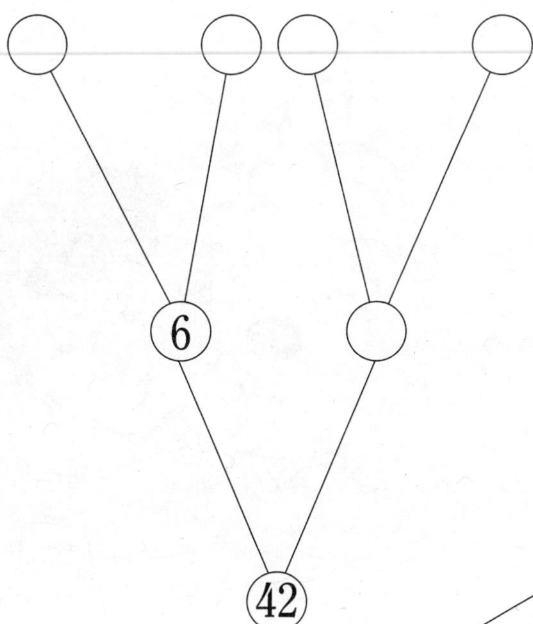

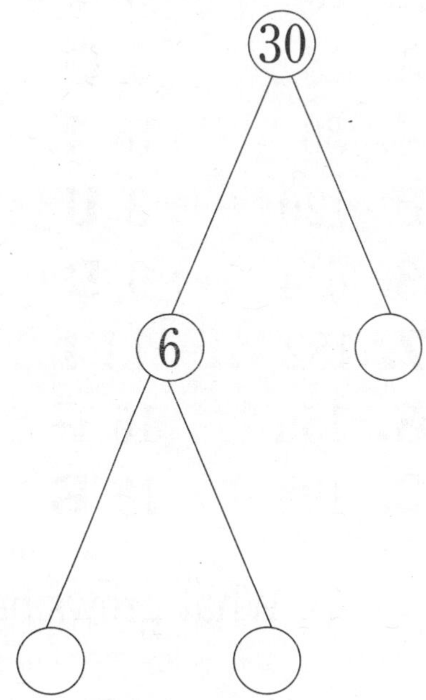

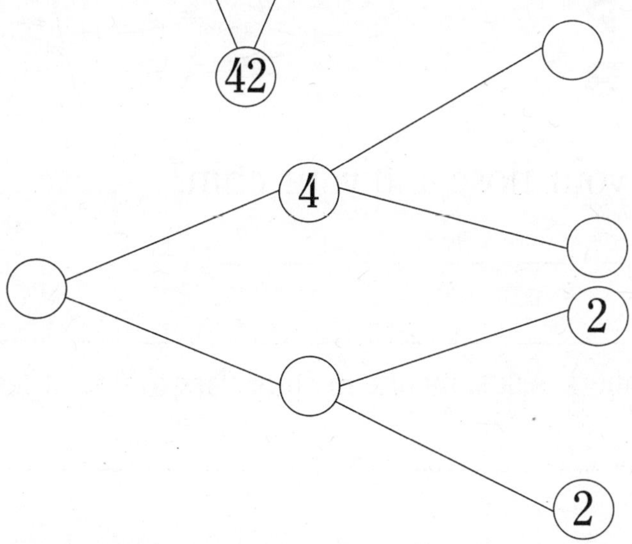

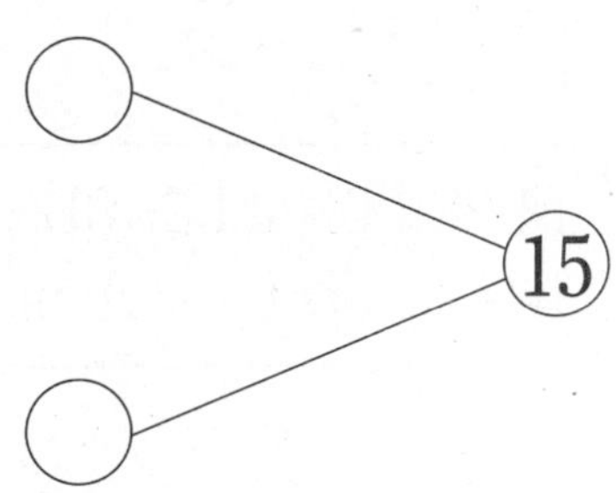

Face Facts

Name ____________________ Date __________

The most common way people recognise each other is by the way they look. Each person has distinct eyes, ears, and other features that set them apart from everyone else. Try answering the wacky riddle below to name another feature people have that sets them apart. Factors will help you find the answer.

DIRECTIONS:
Each number is followed by two possible factors. Circle the letter after the number that is a factor. Write the letters in order from the first problem to the last to solve the riddle.

1.	22	2 **I**	6 **O**
2.	70	5 **T**	15 **A**
3.	48	5 **O**	8 **S**
4.	80	16 **T**	11 **B**
5.	120	3 **U**	13 **E**
6.	644	9 **D**	7 **L**
7.	182	13 **I**	4 **L**
8.	156	16 **F**	4 **P**
9.	198	10 **R**	9 **S**

What grows between your nose and your chin?

__ __'__ "__ __ __ __ __ __"!

SUPER CHALLENGE: Make a list of numbers. Ask someone in your class to find at least two factors for each number.

What Number Am I?

Name ______________________ Date ____________

1 **I am a 2-digit number. The sum of my digits is 9. 3 is one of my factors. I am odd.**

What number am I? ____________

2 **I am a 2-digit number divisible by 4, 6, and 10.**

What number am I? ____________

3 **I am a 2-digit number; 9 is one of my factors. The sum of my digits is 9. I am even.**

What number am I? ____________

4 **I am a 3-digit number divisible by 3 and 11. The sum of my digits is 9.**

What number am I? ____________

5 **I am a 3-digit number less than 150. 5 is a factor of mine. The sum of the digits in my tens and units place is 7.**

What number am I? ____________

6 **I am a 4-digit number3. All four digits of mine are the same. I am divisible by 2 but not by 4.**

What number am I? ____________

Venn, What and Where?

Name ______________________________ Date ______________

Write all the numbers from 1 to 60 on the line below.

____

____

Now choose numbers from the list and place them accurately in the appropriate circles below. Then, tell what the common factors are:

Factors of 24

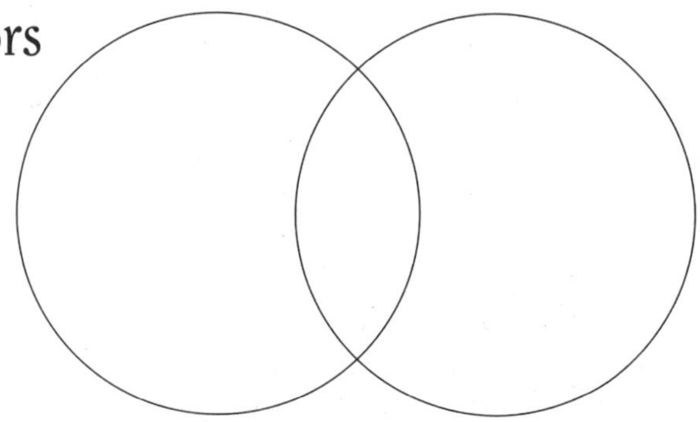

Factors of 36

The common factors are:

____

Factors of 30

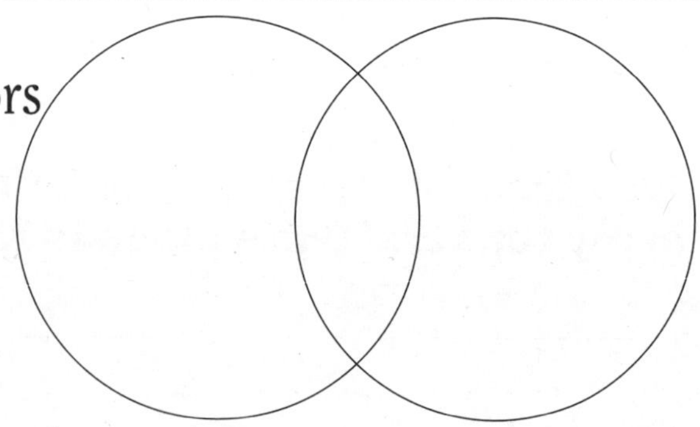

Factors of 60

The common factors are:

____

Factors of 51

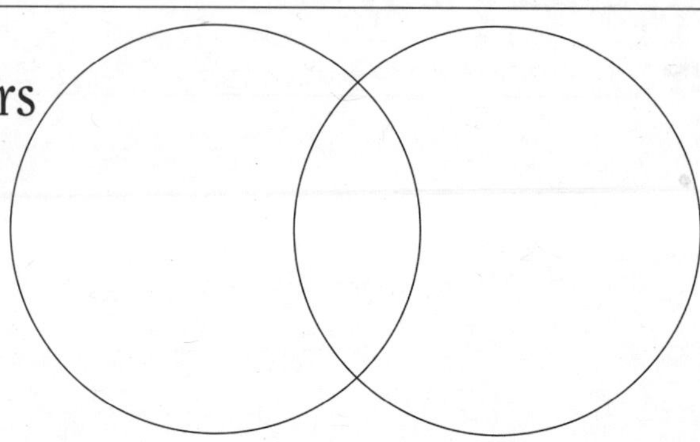

Factors of 13

The common factors are:

____

Multiple Multiples

Name ______________________________ Date ____________

Place the multiples less than or equal to 60 in the appropriate circles below. Then tell what the common multiples are:

Multiples of 4

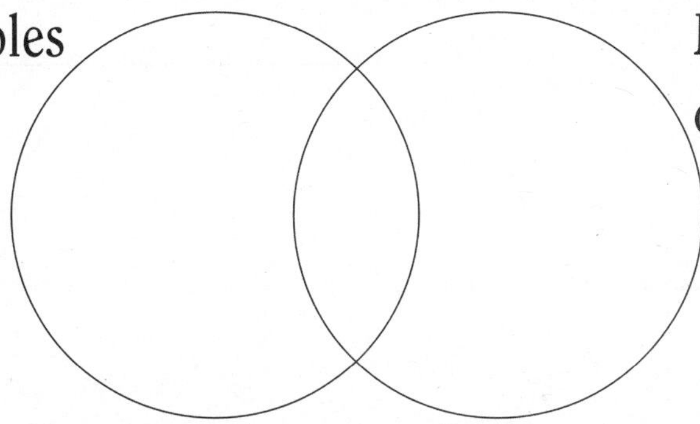

Multiples of 9

The common multiples are: ____________

Multiples of 5

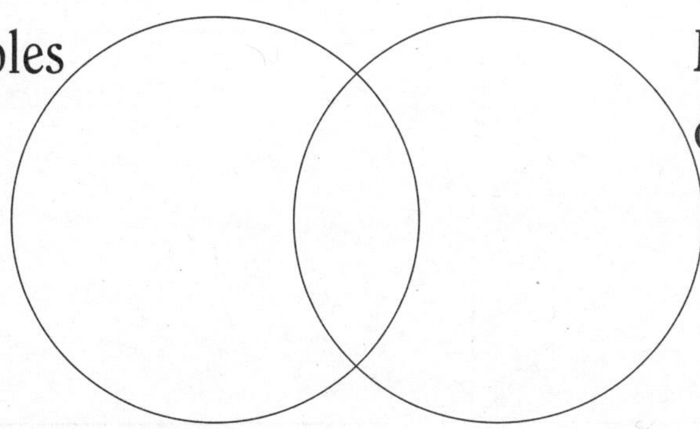

Multiples of 6

The common multiples are: ____________

Multiples of 10

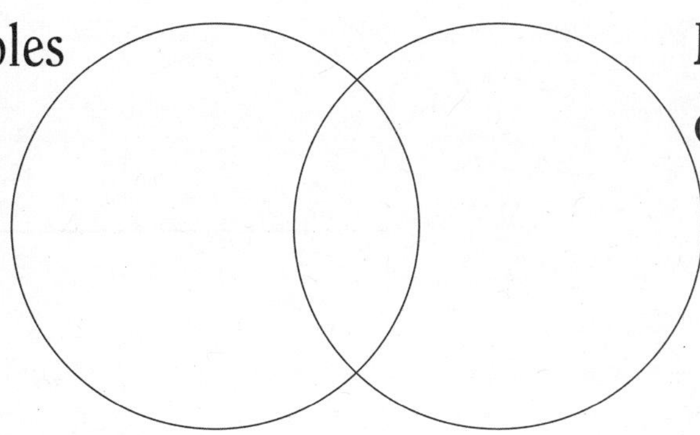

Multiples of 8

The common multiples are: ____________

Pretty Patterns

Name ______________________________ Date ______________

Examine the pattern and draw what comes next.

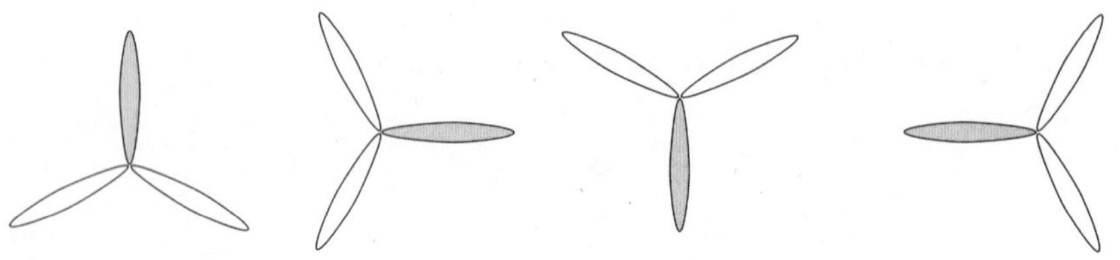

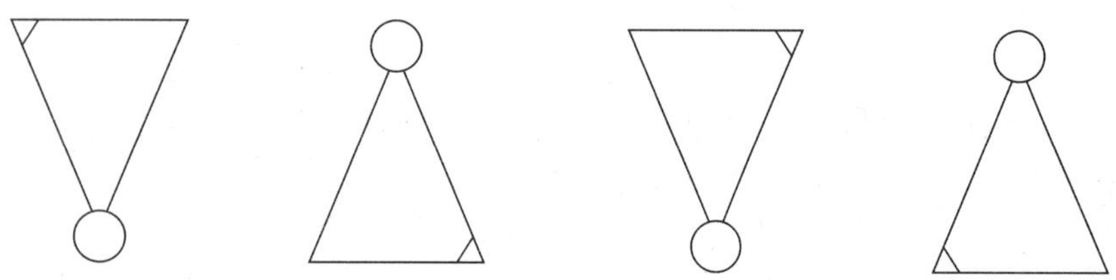

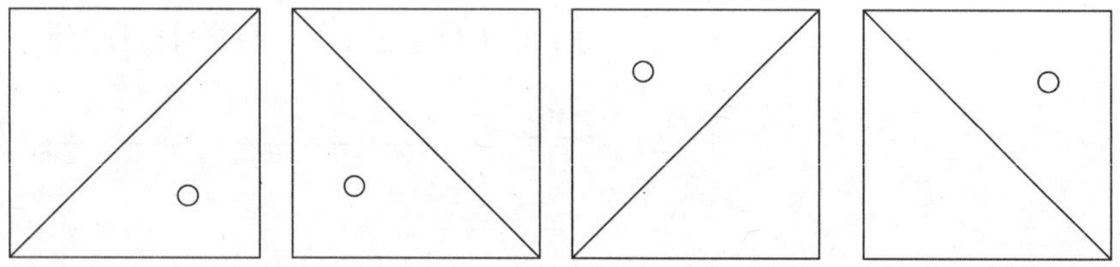

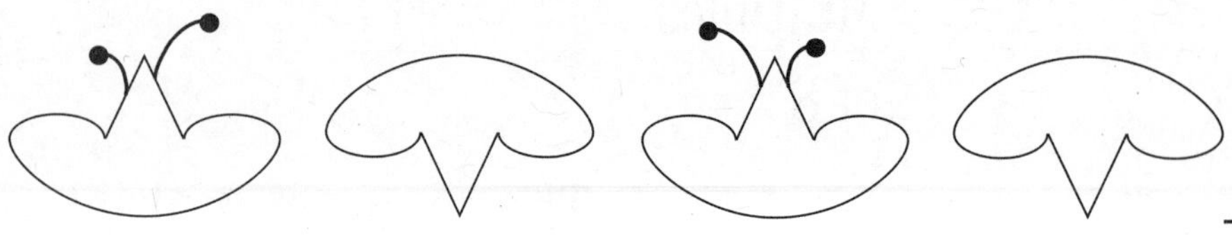

Quater Turns

Name ______________________________ Date ______________

This pattern is made by turning the number 3 by a one-fourth turn, each time.

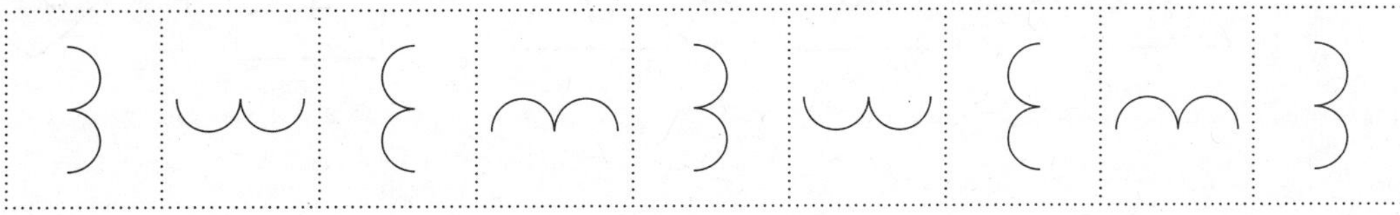

Can you make patterns using the shape given and rotating it by one-fourth turn each time?

Same Thing

Name ______________________________ Date ______________

Fill in the blanks. The first one has been done for you.

24 + ___ + 7 = 35 = 7 + 4 + 24

9 + 11 + 6 = ___ = ___ + ___ + ___

1000 + ___ + 2000 = 10,000 = ___ + ___ + ___

69 × ___ = 138 = ___ × ___

11 × 10 × 3 = ___ = ___ × ___ × ___

4 × 8 + 1 = ___ = 1 + ___ × ___

Hop in Patterns

Name ______________________________ Date ______________

This is part of the 1 to 100 chart. Can you fill in the empty spaces?

A.

1	2	
	12	
	22	23

B.

		80
	89	
98		100

C.

	59	60
		70
78		80

D.

23		
	34	
		45

E.

		44
	53	
62		

F.

	67	
76		78
	87	

Scaling Up

Name ______________________________ Date ____________

Make these drawing bigger by using the grid below to guide you.

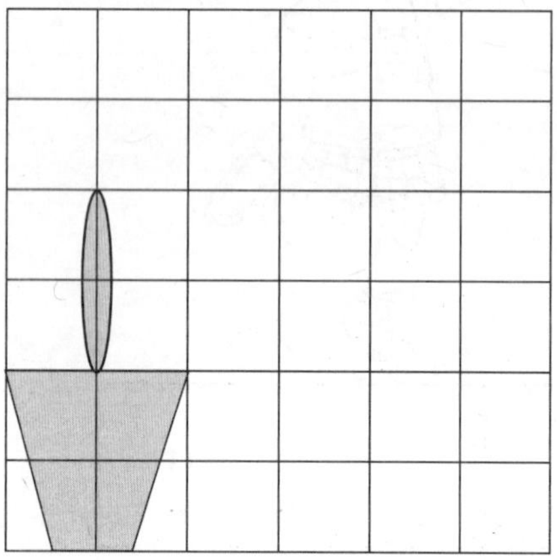

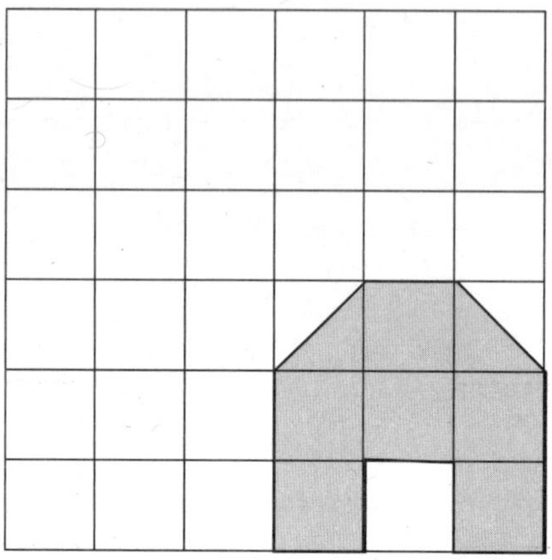

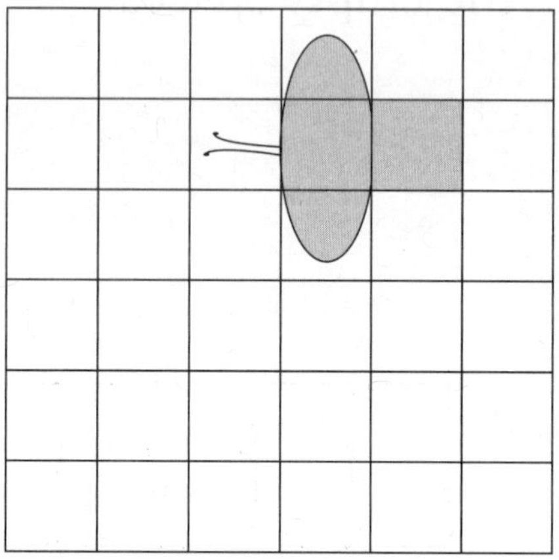

Converting 2D to 3D

Name ____________________ Date __________

Let's make some deep drawings.

Step 1: Choose a point × to right and above the shape

Step 2: Connect the vertices to ×

Step 3: Draw lines parallel to the sides of the shape.

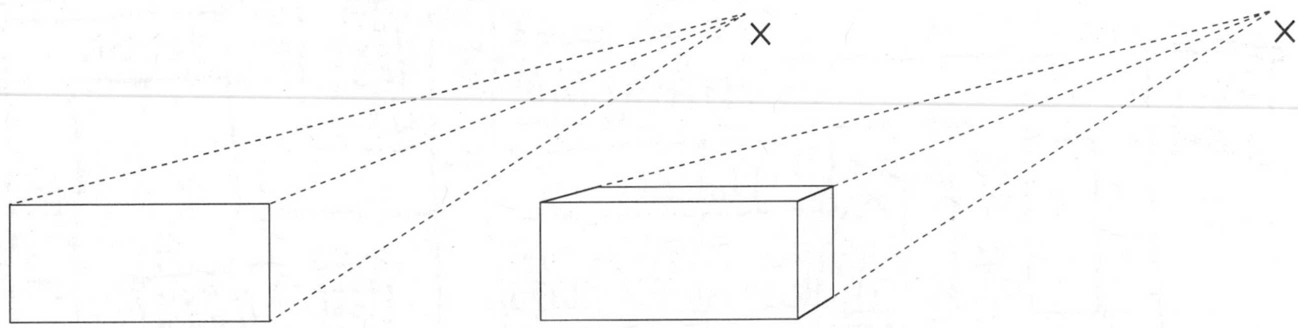

Can you follow the steps and convert these shapes to a deep-drawing. Use one diagram for all the steps.

Scat, Billy Bat!

Name ______________________ Date __________

Billy Bat is lost in the city. Help him get home to his cave. Then, answer these questions that rhyme with 'bat' to find the way.

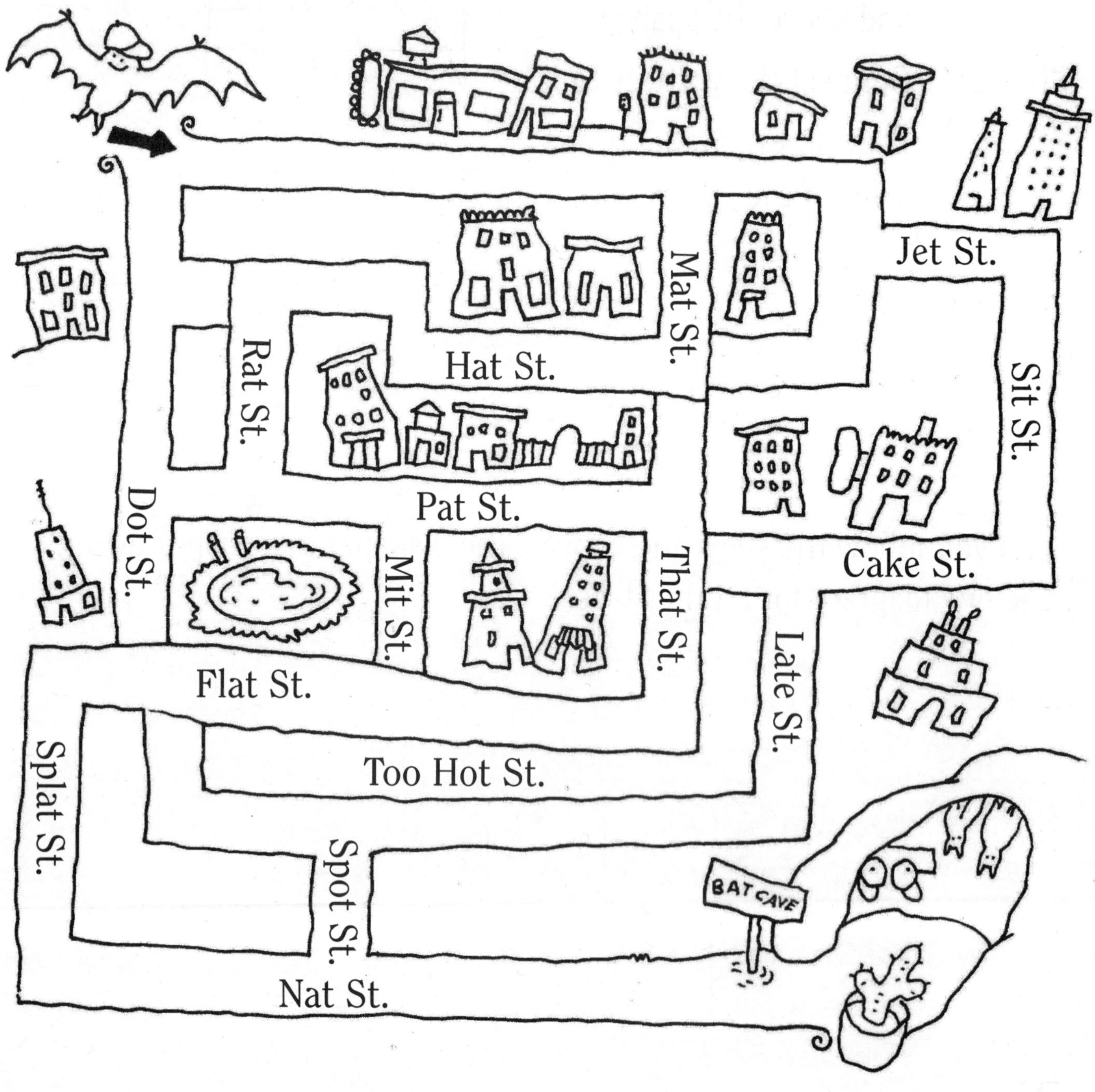

1. As Billy Bat goes from Mat. St. to Hat St. he will turn _________ (left/right)

2. Pat. St. is at a _____________ (45°/90°) angle to That St.

3. The longest street is ____________________ (Hat St. / Nat.St.)

4. A street that Billy Bat takes but does not have a name comes right before _________________St.

5. One street that Billy Bat takes that is not entirely straight is _____________St.

6. The street closest to the cave is ________________St.

7. Billy Bat takes a total of _________________streets with names to reach the cave.

What's Hoppin'?

Name ______________________________ Date ____________

You Answer It!

1. Look at the graph below. Starting at square X, Judy hopped 4 squares up and 3 squares to the right. In which square did she land?

____

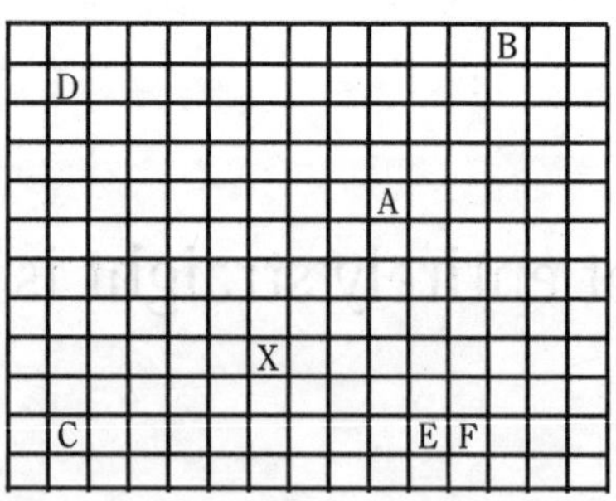

NOTE: Judy and Rudy can hop in vertical and horizontal directions only.

2. Rudy is in square X. Which are the 2 shortest paths he can take to get to square E?

____

____

3. Judy is in square A. Which are the 2 shortest paths she can take to get to square E?

____

____

4. Find the 2 shortest paths to get from square X to square D.

____

____

5. Find 3 paths to get from square D to square E. Does each path contain the same total number of squares?

____

____

6. Starting at square X, Rudy hopped 6 squares up and 5 squares to the left. How many squares is he from square D?

____

____

Cubes with a Views

Name ______________________________ Date ______________

Write how many cubes are in each of these arrangements. Then, match them to their top views by drawing lines.

1. 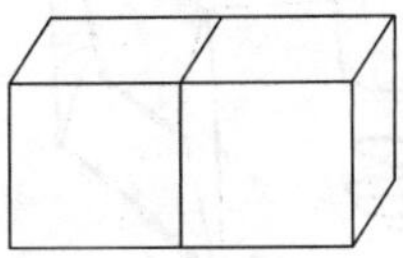 _______ cubes

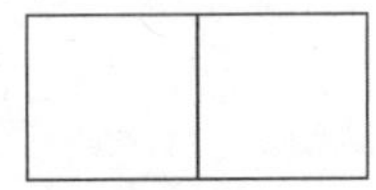

A.

2. 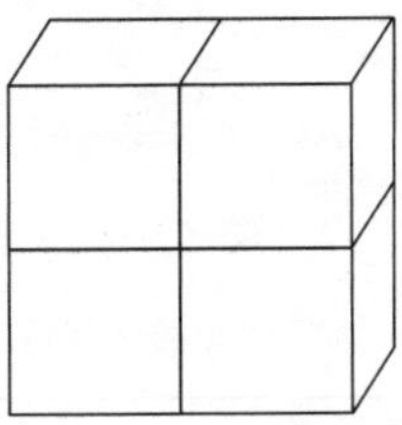 _______ cubes

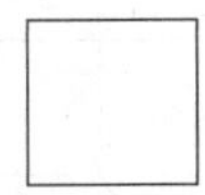

B.

3. 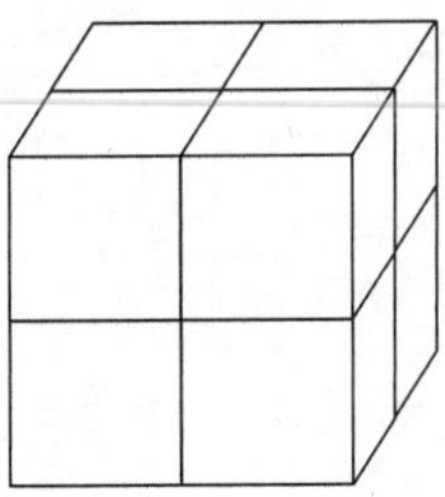 _______ cubes

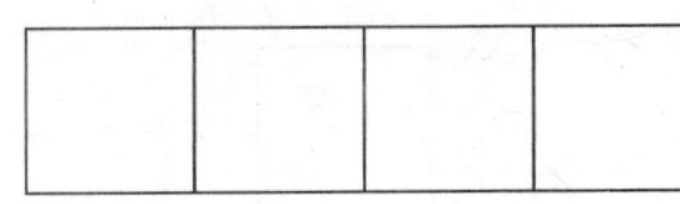

C.

4. 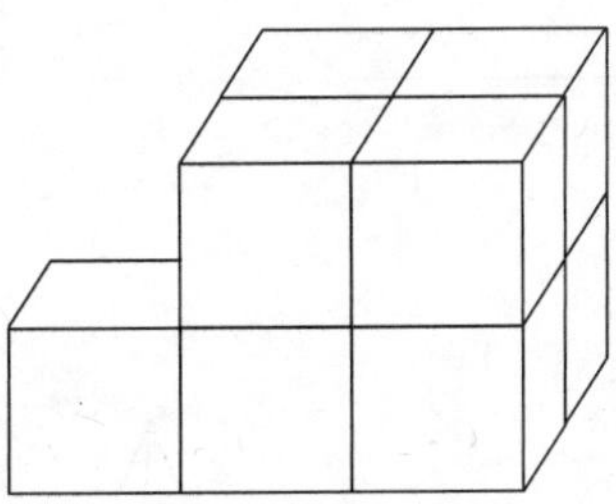 _______ cubes

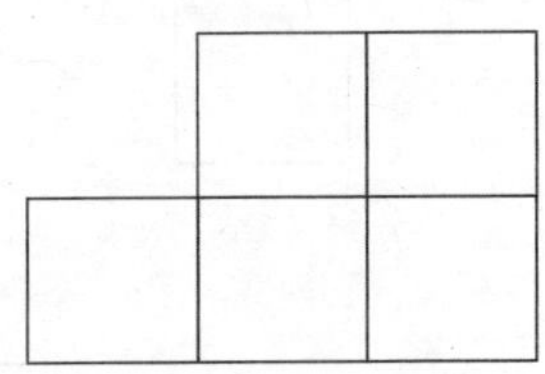

D.

5. 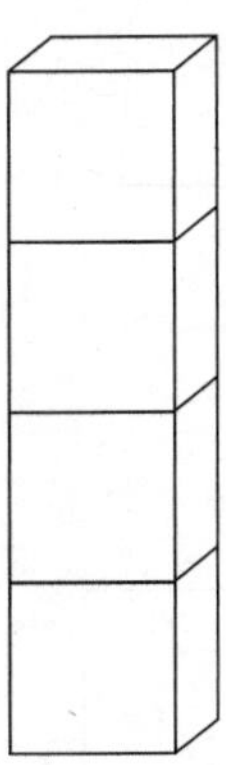 _______ cubes

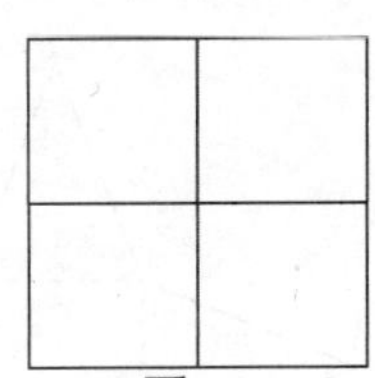

E.

SUPER CHALLENGE: Do any of these of the name side view? which ones?

Making 3D Shapes

Name ______________________________ Date ____________

Match the following nets to the 3D shapes they represent by drawing lines.

1. 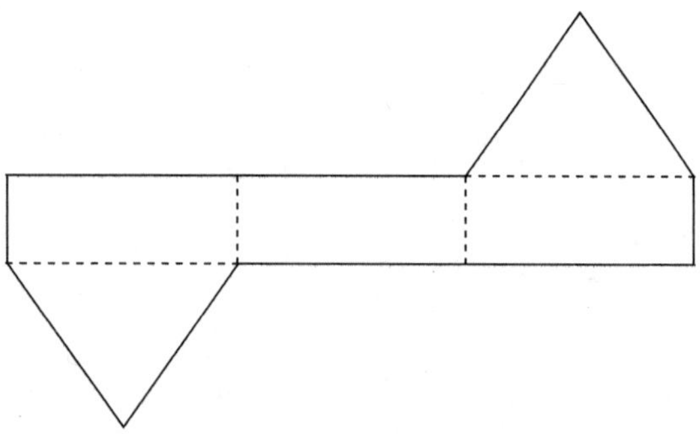

2. 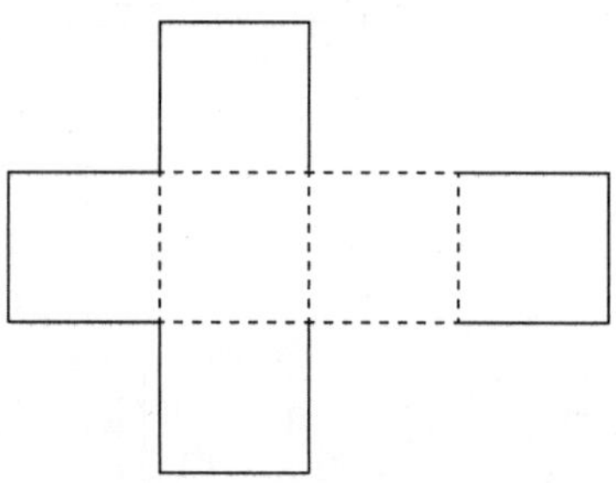

3. 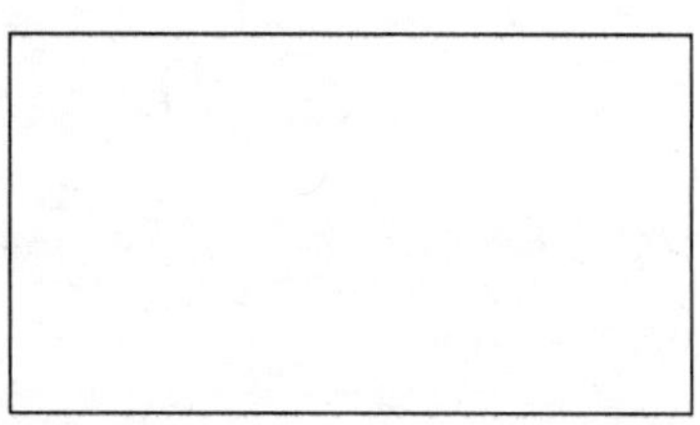

4. 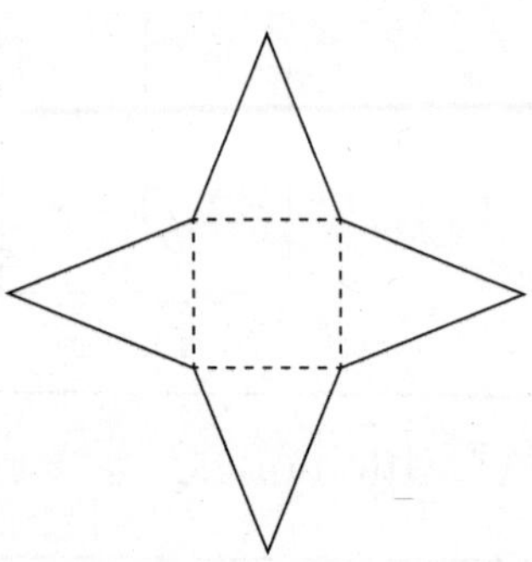

A. 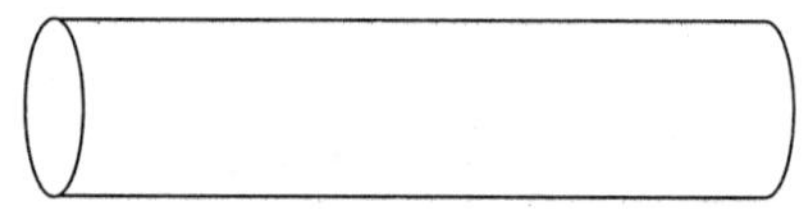

B. 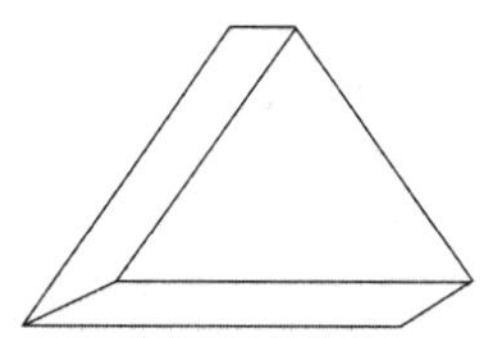

C. 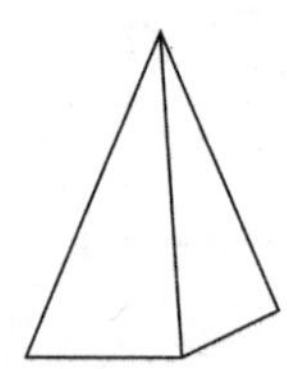

D. 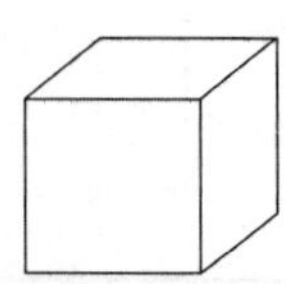

Ring of Stars

Name ______________________________ Date ______________

Form a star polygon by connecting the dots beside the decimals inside the pentagon. Begin with the smallest decimal and continue connecting the dots until you reach the largest decimal. The first and last lines have been drawn for you.

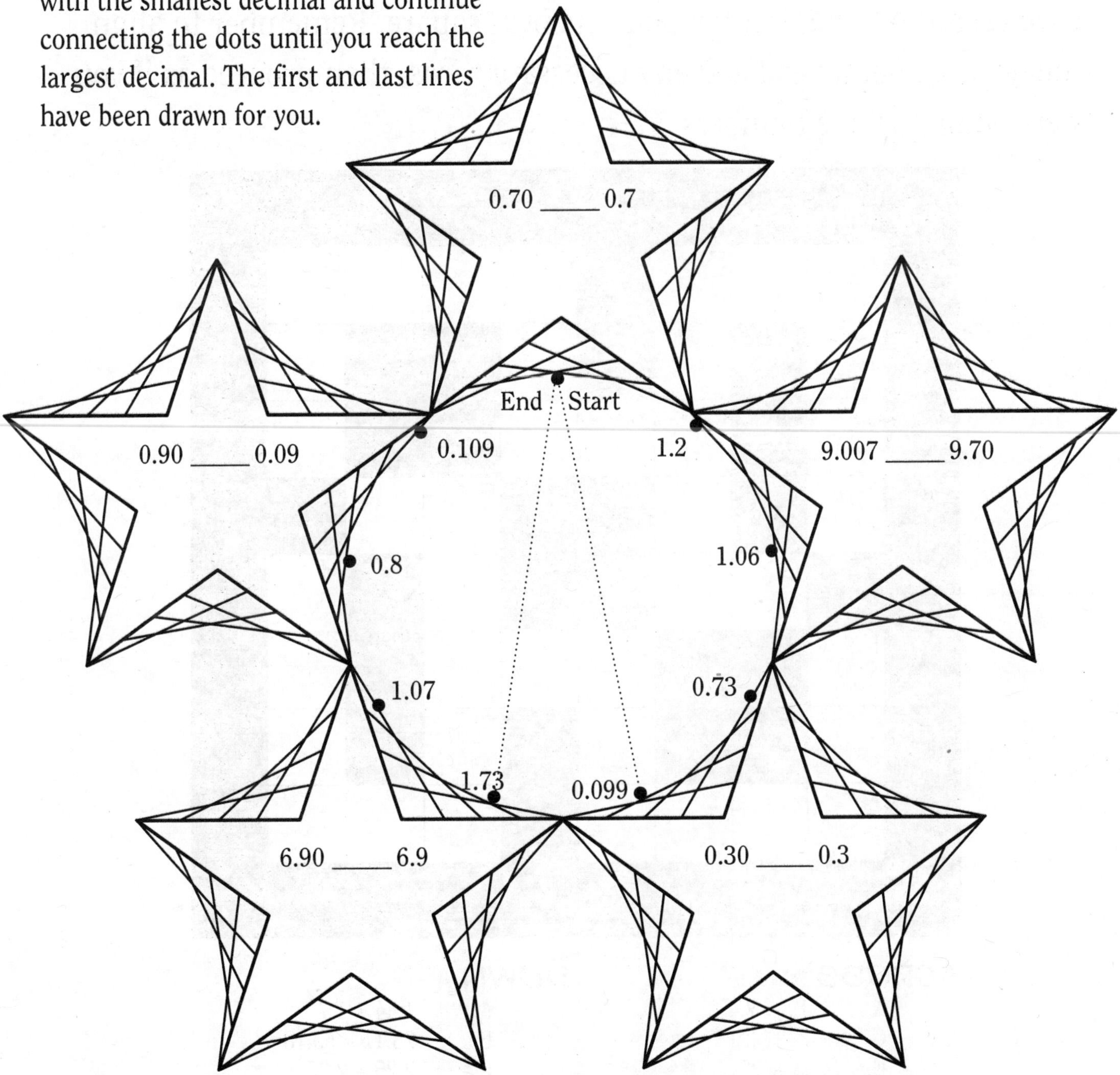

Taking It Further: Compare each pair of decimals inside the outer stars by writing <, >, or = on each blank line. If the decimals inside the star are equivalent, color the star blue. If the decimals inside the star are not equivalent, color the star red. Finish the design by coloring the rest of the shapes with the colors of your choice.

Across-and-Down Decimals

Name ______________________________ Date ______________

Complete the crossnumber puzzle as if it were a crossword puzzle. Give each digit and decimal point its own square. Remember to align the decimal points and add any necessary zeros, then proceed as if you were adding whole numbers.

ACROSS

A. 1.3 + 2.4
C. 2.2 + 2.18
E. .3 + .25
F. .3 + .3
G. .56 + .34
J. .4 + .17
K. 6.93 + .23
L. 1.18 + 3.12

DOWN

A. 1.44 + 1.7
B. 23.11 + 53.18
C. 2.25 + 2.25
D. 6.5 + 1.6
F. .1604 + .11
H. 20.8 + 3.5
I. 1.36 + .34
J. .2 + .16

Change Arranger

Name ______________________ Date ____________

Vidur has gone to a second-hand toy shop. When he tries of find out the amount of change, he counts on from the price. Start with the coins that have the least value. Write the change from these purchases.

1. LAWN GAME

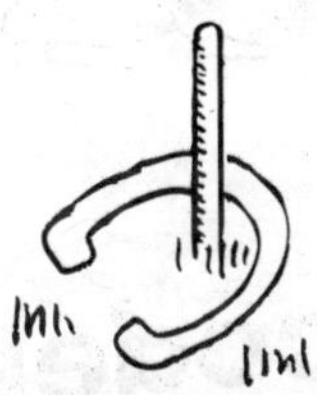

AMOUNT GIVEN	₹ 5.00
PRICE	₹ 3.45
CHANGE	______

2. YO-YO

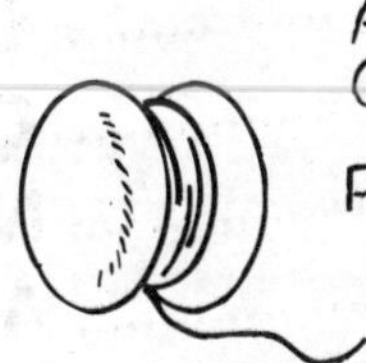

AMOUNT GIVEN	₹ 3.00
PRICE	₹ 2.77
CHANGE	______

3. BIKE HELMET

AMOUNT GIVEN	₹10.00
PRICE	₹ 7.55
CHANGE	______

4. SOAP BUBBLES

AMOUNT GIVEN	₹ 2.00
PRICE	₹ 1.52
CHANGE	______

5. VIDEO GAME

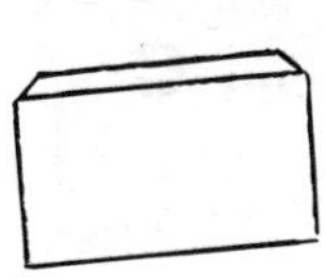

AMOUNT GIVEN	₹ 20.00
PRICE	₹ 7.30
CHANGE	______

6. BABY DINOSAUR

AMOUNT GIVEN	₹10.00
PRICE	₹ 6.49
CHANGE	______

7. SUNGLASSES

AMOUNT GIVEN	₹ 4.00
PRICE	₹ 3.68
CHANGE	______

8. BACKPACK

AMOUNT GIVEN	₹ 20.00
PRICE	₹ 9.35
CHANGE	______

9. JUMP ROPE

AMOUNT GIVEN	₹ 4.00
PRICE	₹ 3.17
CHANGE	______

10. MARKERS

AMOUNT GIVEN	₹ 5.00
PRICE	₹ 2.43
CHANGE	______

A Sick Riddle

Name ______________________________ Date ______________

Riddle: Why do people with colds get plenty of exercise?

Find the answers. Then use the Decoder to solve the riddle by filling in the blanks at the bottom of the page.

1. What is the perimeter of this square? 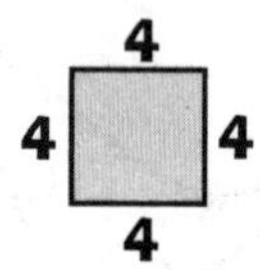

______

2. What is the perimeter of this rectangle? 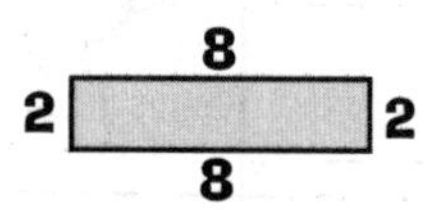

______

3. What is the perimeter of this triangle? 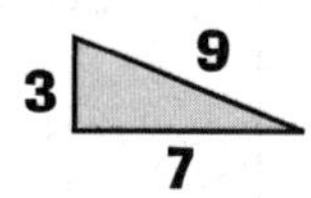

______

4. What is the perimeter of a square that is 10 cm long on one side?
______

5. A square's perimeter is 48 cm. How long is one side of the square?
______

6. A triangle with three equal sides has a perimeter of 27 cm. How long is one side of the triangle? ______

7. Each side of a pentagon is 11 cm long. What is the pentagon's perimeter? ______

8. What is the perimeter of this shape? ______

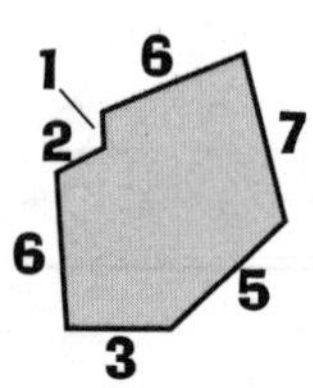

9. A card is 11 cm long and 8 inches wide.
What is the card's perimeter? ______

10. A lawn is 23 metre long and 14 metre wide. What is the lawn's perimeter? ______

Decoder

19 .... O
74 m .... Q
30 .... N
25 .... A
38 cm I
12 cm .... S
40 cm X
9 cm .... N
15 .... B
74 cm .... R
16 .... E
10 cm .... D
20 .... R
22 .... A
32 cm L
37 cm .... M
40 cm .... U
55 cm .... S
15 C

THE ___ ___ ___ ___ ___ ___ ___ ___ ___ ___.
9 2 8 3 5 1 7 10 4 6

Tile Designs

Name ______________________ Date ____________

Make four different designs on this dot sheet. If the area of a tile

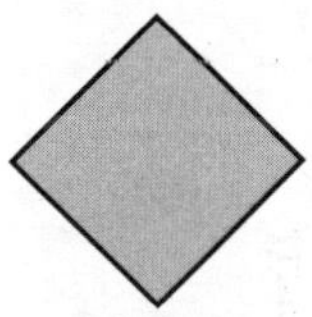 is 1 sq. unit, what is the total area of each of your designs?

Design 1 has been done for you.

Design 1 : 1.5 sq. units

Design 2 :

Design 3 :

Design 4 :

Math's Got It Covered

Name ______________________ Date ____________

This football player sure has a lot of ground to cover. Just how much exactly? Look at the picture and answer the questions. Don't forget to mention the units!

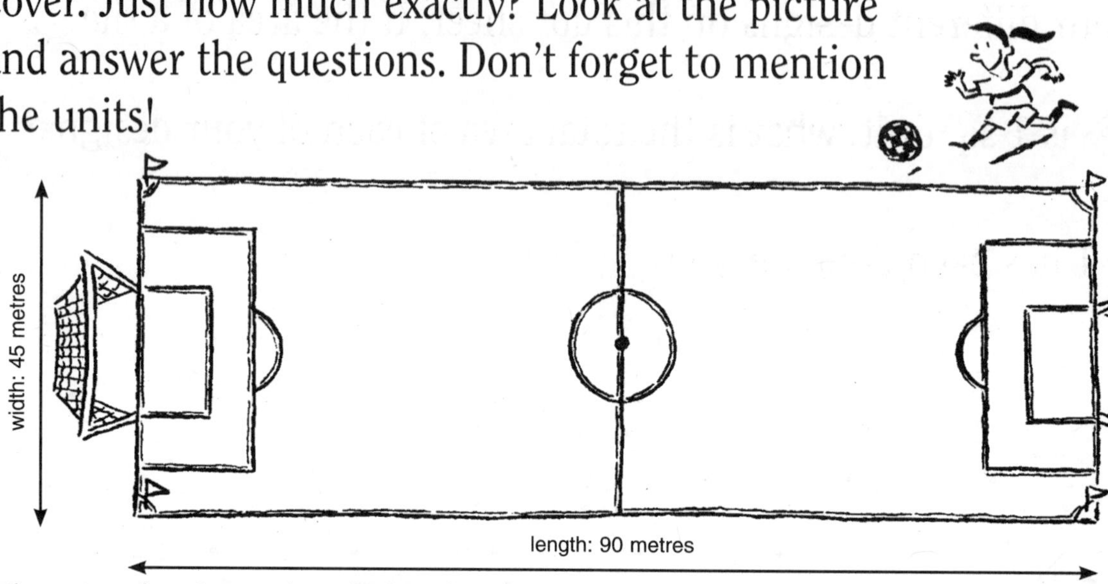

1. **What is the length of the field?** ________
   What is the width of the field? ________
   What is the perimeter of the field? ________
   What is the area of the field? ________

2. **What is the perimeter of half of the field?** ________
   What is the area of half of the field? ________

3. **Imagine a field with a length of 130 metres and a width of 75 metres.**
   What is the perimeter of that field? ________
   What is the area of that field? ________

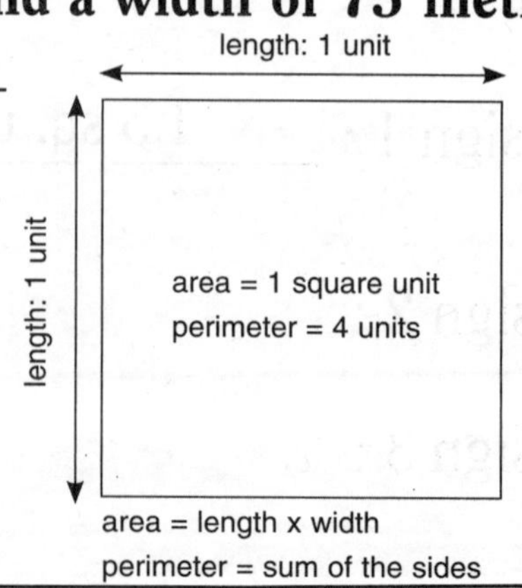

SUPER CHALLENGE: All-Star Math!
Is the perimeter of half the field what you expected? Why or why not?

Break the Ice With Perimeter and Area

Name ______________________ Date ____________

Jessie is building ice skating rinks for her friends. She measures the size of each rink in two ways—**perimeter** and **area**. Perimeter tells the measurement **around** the rink. Area tells how many square units fit **inside** each rink. Some rinks have the same area but different perimeters. Try some building yourself!

You Need:
square crackers biscuits or square counters

Here's the rink Jesse built for Shawn. Its area is 4. Its perimeter is 8.

What to Do:

Use the square crackers to help you answer the questions. Then draw how the crackers look.

1. Shawn wants a bigger rink. He wants it to have a perimeter of 12 and an area of 8. What can you add to Shawn's rink? Draw what it will look like.

2. Gil also wants a rink with a perimeter of 12. But he wants it to be square. What will it look like? What will its area be? Draw what it will look like.

3. The area of Rita's rink is 12. Its perimeter is 14. What does her rink look like? Draw it.

4. Sonia wants her rink to have an area of 16. She says it can be shaped like a square or a rectangle. What could the rink look like? What will its perimeter be? Draw it.

5. José wants a rink with an area of 24. It can be any shape. What are some of the shapes it could be? What are their perimeters? Draw one example.

SUPER CHALLENGE: Draw a shape whose perimeter and area are the same number.

Graph Drafter

Name ______________________________ Date ______________

A line graph shows how something changes over time. This line graph shows temperature changes during a year in New York City. Use the graph to answer the questions below.

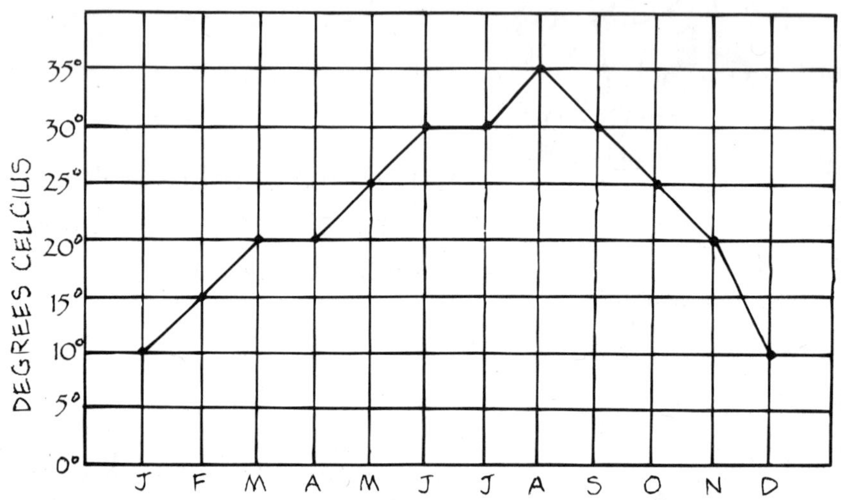

SUGGESTION: SHORTEN THE NAMES, LIKE JAN, FEB, AUG, SEP, OCT, NOV.

1. WHAT 2 MONTHS WERE THE COLDEST? ______________
2. WHAT WAS THE TEMPERATURE OF THE HOTTEST MONTH? ______________
3. WHAT MONTHS WERE 70°? ______________
4. ANY TEMPERATURE CHANGE BETWEEN JAN. AND FEB.? ______________
5. WAS THE TEMPERATURE EVER WARMER THAN AUGUST? ______________
6. DID IT BECOME COLDER OR WARMER IN JUNE? ______________
7. DID THE TEMPERATURE RISE OR FALL IN OCTOBER? ______________
8. WHAT MONTH IS THE 5th MONTH? ______________
9. HOW MANY DEGREES BETWEEN 15° AND 35°? ______________

Decibel Tester

Name ______________________ Date ____________

A bar graph is used to compare information.This bar graph shows the relative loudness of sound measured in decibels (dB). One decibel is the smallest difference between sound heard by the human ear. A 100-decibel sound is 10 times louder than a 10-decibel sound. A 100-decibel sound is painful!

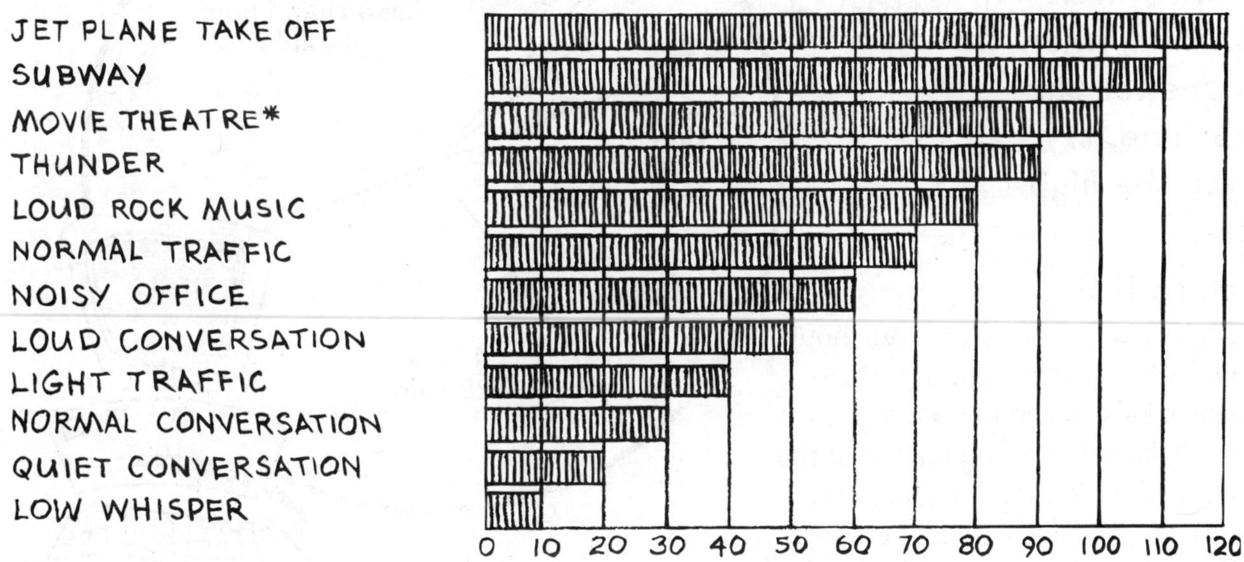

* SPEAKER VOLUMES IN A DIGITAL THEATER SOUND SYSTEM.

HOW MUCH LOUDER IN DECIBELS IS...

1. LOUD CONVERSATION THAN QUIET CONVERSATION? ____________
2. NORMAL TRAFFIC THAN LIGHT TRAFFIC? ____________
3. A MOVIE THEATRE DIGITAL SOUND SYSTEM THAN LOUD ROCK MUSIC? ____________
4. A SUBWAY TRAIN THAN THUNDER? ____________
5. A NOISY OFFICE THAN QUIET CONVERSATION? ____________
6. WHAT IS THE LOUDEST SOUND SHOWN ON THE GRAPH? ____________
7. HOW MANY DECIBELS IS THE LOUDEST SOUND? ____________

Great Game Graph!

Name ______________________________ Date ______________

How much time do kids really spend playing video games? Read the circle graph to find out. Then, when you answer the questions, try to get the high score!

How Long Kids Play Video Games Each Day

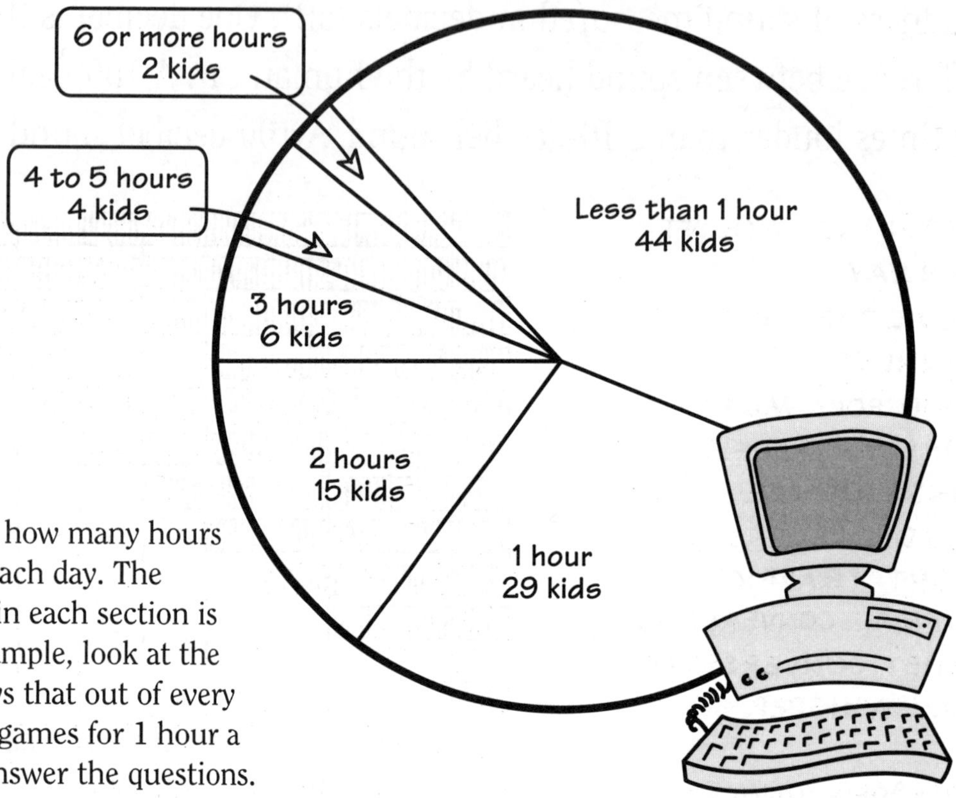

What to Do:

The circle graph shows how many hours kids play video games each day. The number of kids shown in each section is out of 100 kids. For example, look at the bottom section. It shows that out of every 100 kids, 29 play video games for 1 hour a day. Use the graph to answer the questions.

1. How many kids out of 100 play video games for 2 hours a day? ______________

2. How many hours a day do 6 out of 100 kids play video games? ______________

3. For how long does the largest group of kids play video games each day? ______________

4. For how long does the smallest group of kids play video games each day? ______________

5. Do more or less than $\frac{1}{2}$ of the kids play video games for less than 1 hour a day?

____

6. Think of the amount of time you play video games each day. What is the section of the graph where you would be? ______________________________

Multiplying & Dividing

Name ______________________ Date ____________

Using the digits in the box, write the answer to each number riddle in the form of an equation. Digits appear only once in an answer.

8 1 4 7 3

1 **The product of a 1-digit number and a 2-digit number is 284.**

What are the numbers? ______________

2 **The product of two 2-digit numbers, plus a number, is 3,355.**

What are the numbers? ______________

3 **The product of a 3-digit number and a 1-digit number, minus another 1-digit number, is 1,137.**

What are the numbers? ______________

4 **The product of a 2-digit number and a 3-digit number is between 13,000 and 14,000.**

What are the numbers? ______________

5 **When a 3-digit number is divided by a 2-digit number, the quotient is between 5 and 6.**

What are the numbers? ______________

6 **When a 2-digit prime number is divided by another 2-digit prime number, the quotient is nearly 5.**

What are the numbers? ______________

Changing Shapes

Name ______________________________ Date ______________

Riddle: How did the square become a triangle?

To find the answer to the riddle, solve the multiplication problems here. (Don't forget units.) Then, match each product with a letter in the Key below. Write the correct letters on the blanks below.

1. Arvind has 2 apples. Tarun has 2 times as many apples as Arvind has. How many apples does Tarun have? _______
2. Kendra has 3 books. Paula has 3 times as many books as Kendra has. How many books does Paula have? _______
3. Kabir has 5 times as many caps as Wasim has. Wasim has 5 caps. How many caps does Kabir have? _______
4. Jorge has 10 oranges. Wendy has 2 times as many oranges as Jorge has. How many oranges does Wendy have? _______
5. Maya has 6 times as many coats as Shanti has. Shanti has 5 coats. How many coats does Maya have? _______
6. Debbie has 9 pairs of shoes. How many shoes does she have in all? _______
7. Mayank has 8 bunches of bananas. Each bunch has 7 bananas. How many bananas does he have in all? _______
8. Lakshya has 11 times as many pencils as Aarish has. Aarish has 11 pencils. How many pencils does Lakshya have? _______
9. Aarohi has 6 video games. Atharv has 8 times as many video games as Aarohi has. How many video games do Aarohi and Atharv have in all? _______
10. Kaavya has 7 chairs. Kopal has 7 times as many chairs as Kaavya has. How many more chairs does Kopal have than Kaavya? _______

Key

4 apples	T
20 oranges	C
18 shoes	N
56 bananas	C
111 pencils	I
54 video games	E
48 video games	F
30 coats	U
2 apples	S
42 chairs	A
15 bananas	K
9 books	R
25 caps	R
121 pencils	O
40 coats	B

Riddle Answer: **IT** ___ ___ ___ ___ ___ ___ ___ ___ ___ ___.

(7) (5) (1) (10) (4) (8) (3) (6) (9) (2)

Caught in the Web

Name ______________________ Date __________

Why did the spider join the baseball team?

What To Do

To find the answer to the riddle, solve the multiplication problems. Then, match each product with a letter in the Key below. Write the correct letters on the blanks below.

1. 1,000 x 11 = ______
2. 2,000 x 12 = ______
3. 3,000 x 10 = ______
4. 4,000 x 14 = ______
5. 5,000 x 20 = ______
6. 6,000 x 24 = ______
7. 7,000 x 30 = ______
8. 8,000 x 32 = ______
9. 9,000 x 40 = ______
10. 7,500 x 50 = ______

Key

56,000	H	65,000	M	30,000	C
11,000	I	1,44,000	T	3,75,000	C
2,65,000	B	25,000	N	10,000	Y
3,60,000	F	2,56,000	L	1,00,000	A
2,10,000	E	90,000	Q	24,000	S

Riddle Answer: TO ___ ___ ___ ___ ___ "___ ___ ___ ___ ___"

3 5 6 10 4   9 8 1 7 2

Biting Riddle

Name ________________________ Date ____________

Riddle: What has teeth but cannot bite?

Decoder

20 remainder 10. **C**
8 .... **E**
30 remainder 40.. **A**
7 remainder 9 ..... **F**
11 .... **K**
6 remainder 56 .. **B**
40 remainder 30. **O**
4 .... **T**
12 .... **I**
33 remainder 12 **M**
32 remainder 12 . **L**
9 remainder 7 ..... **Y**
8 remainder 50 .. **N**
30 remainder 23 **D**
9 remainder 50 .. **C**
6 remainder 58 .. **S**
5 remainder 2 .... **Q**
6 .... **W**
5 .... **A**

Find each quotient. Then use the Decoder to solve the riddle by filling in the spaces at the bottom of the page.

1. 100 ÷ 25 = ____________
2. 330 ÷ 16 = ____________
3. 407 ÷ 37 = ____________
4. 560 ÷ 84 = ____________
5. 646 ÷ 71 = ____________
6. 950 ÷ 100 = ____________
7. 1,000 ÷ 200 = ____________
8. 1,200 ÷ 36 = ____________
9. 1,540 ÷ 50 = ____________
10. 270 ÷ 6 = ____________

___ ___ ___ ___ ___
7 2 10 8 4

Pack-Up

Name ______________________ Date ____________

How many centimetre cubes can be packed in the boxes below.

1. 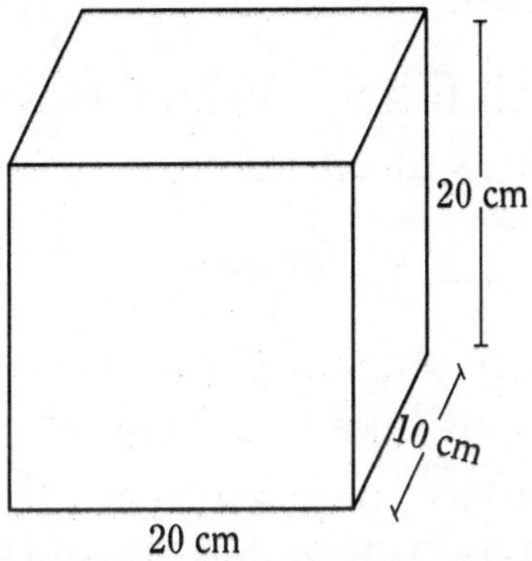

2. 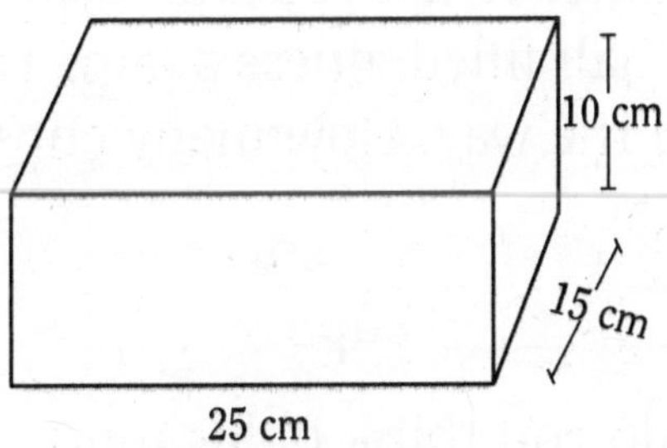

3. 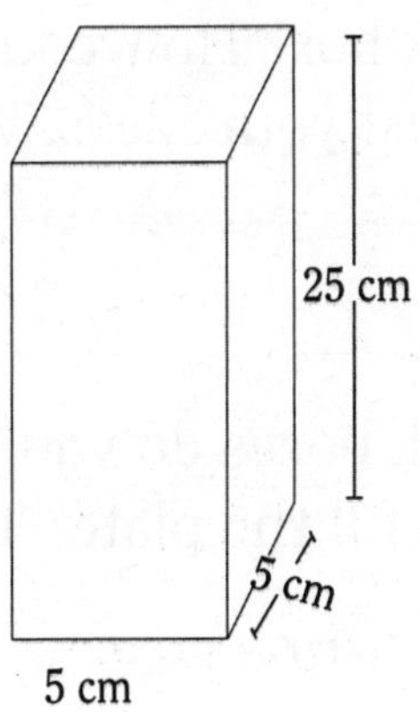

4. 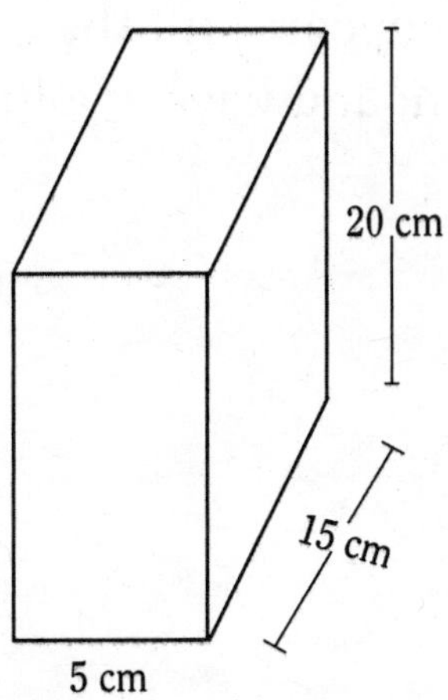

Volume Pops Up Everywhere!

Name ______________________________ Date ____________

Look around the room. Do you see any of the shapes shown here?

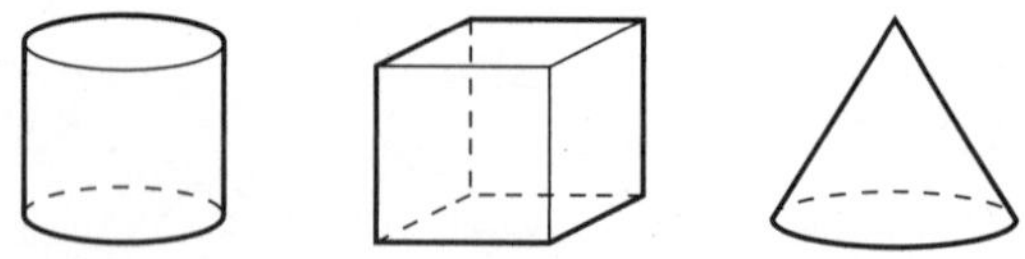

Cylinder Cube Cone

These shapes are three-dimensional. That means that they are solid—you can touch them with your hands. (You can't hold a two-dimensional shape like a circle, square, or triangle.) We measure three-dimensional shapes in a special way—using volume. Volume tells how much the shape can hold inside.

Ready to learn about volume? Let's go!

You Need:
A bag of unpopped popcorn
ice cream cone
empty drink box with top cut off
empty yogurt/curd cup
a thaali/plate

1. Start with the cone and the yogurt cup. How many cones do you think it will take to fill the cup with popcorn?

   __________ cones

   Fill the cone with popcorn. Then pour it into the cup. Keep filling the cup until you think it's half filled.

   Do you want to change your guess?

   New guess: __________ **cones**

   Now finish filling the cup. How many cones did it take?

   __________ cones

2. How many cups of popcorn do you think it will take to fill the plate? Start pouring popcorn from the cup to the plate. When you think the plate is half filled, guess again. Then fill it all the way. How many cups did it take?

   __________ cups

3. Which do you think holds more, the cup or the drink box? How could you find out? Test your ideas. Which holds more?

   ____

4. How many drink boxes do you think it would take to fill the plate? Try it.

   __________ drink boxes

Now pop the popcorn, fill the cone with ice cream, and have a volume party!

Answer Key

Page 5
1. 3,462; **2.** 98,724; **3.** 8,749
4. 1,28,467; **5.** 6,17,823; **6.** 6,18,397

Page 6
1. thousands; **2.** 6; **3.** tens; **4.** 7; **5.** 0; **6.** ten crores; **7.** crores;
8. 7,27,912; **9.** 48,47,266; **10.** 44,67,32,011
How do skunks measure length?
In "SCENT"IMETERS

Page 7
Answers will vary.

Page 8
1. 9,875; **2.** 12,346; **3.** 93,876
4. 13,579; **5.** 9,51,876; **6.** 1,23,648

Page 9

Page 10
Answers will vary. Check to make sure students' drawings have 7 sides.

Page 11

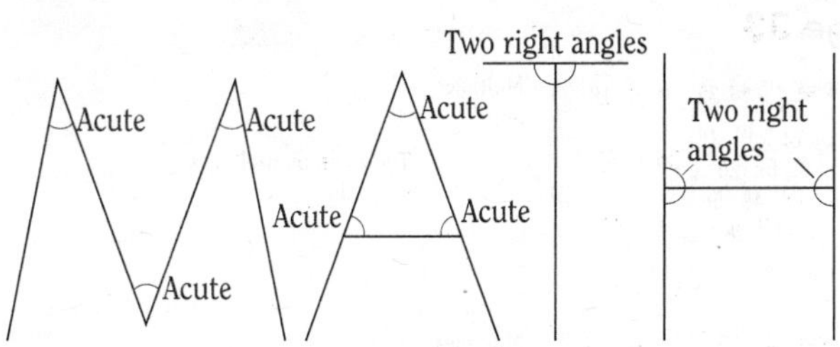

Page 12
1. railway signal; **2.** ironing board; **3.** gas mask;
4. cash register; **5.** ear muffs; **6.** ballpoint pen
7. hearing aid; **8.** windshield wiper

Page 13
1. less than 90°; **2.** exactly 90°; **3.** greater than 90°;
4. less than 90°; **5.** greater than 90° **6.** 180°;
7. exactly 90° **8.** greater than 90°

Page 14
1. 90°; **2.** 60°; **3.** 20°; **4.** 45°; **5.** 165°

Pages 15
1. A: 4 sq. units; B: 4 sq. units; C: 3 sq. units;
C has the least area.

2. A: 5 sq. units; B: 5 sq. units; C: 4 sq. units;
C has the least area.

3. A: 8 sq. units; B: 6 sq. units; C: 8 sq. units;
B has the least area.

4. A: 8 sq. units; B: 8 sq. units; C: 7 sq. units;
C has the least area.

Page 16
1. 4; 2 sq. units; 2 sq. units; 4 sq. units;
2. 4; 2 sq. units; 6 sq. units; 8 sq. units;
3. 8; 4 sq. units; 4 sq. units; 8 sq. units;
4. 8; 4 sq. units; 8 sq. units; 12 sq. units;

Page 17
1. perimeter; **2.** area; **3.** perimeter; **4.** perimeter;
5. area; 6. perimeter

Page 18
Answers will vary. Check to make sure the figures each have 4 sides and that the lengths of the sides add up to the given number.

Page 19
Colour: a) 1 part; b) 6 parts; c) 4 suns; d) 8 stars;
e) 2 moons; f) 3 planets

Page 20

T	H	E	Y	A	L	R	E	A	D	Y
1/5	3/8	4/6	6/8	1/2	2/9	2/3	4/6	1/2	1/3	6/8

H	A	V	E	B	I	L	L	S.
3/8	1/2	5/6	4/6	6/12	3/4	2/9	2/9	3/5

Page 21
1. 1/2; **2.** 1/8; **3.** 1/4; **4.** 1/4; **5.** 1/2; **6.** 1/6
7. 1/2; **8.** 1/2; **9.** 3/4; **10.** 1/4; **11.** 1/2

Page 22
Here are six ways to make whole candy bars out of the fraction pieces. Your students may find more.

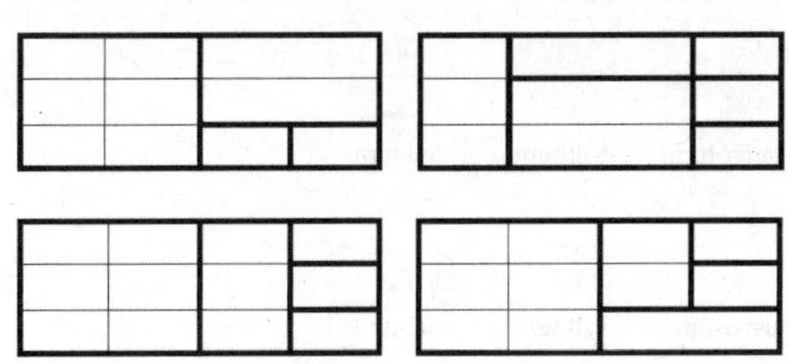

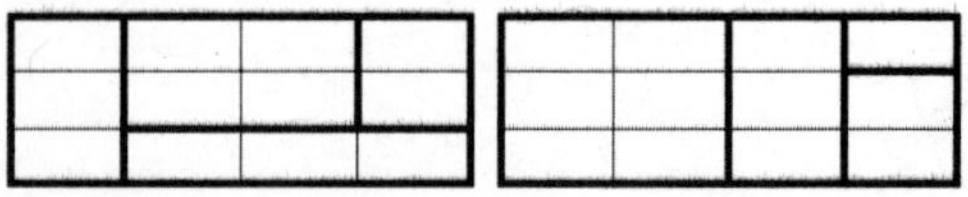

Page 23

1. 1/4; **2.** 1/3; **3.** 1/3; **4.** 1/2; **5.** 1/2
6. 1/4; **7.** 1/3; **8.** 1/2; **9.** 1/4; **10.** 1/4
11. 1/4; **12.** 1/3

Page 24

$\frac{3}{6}$ Blue	$\frac{2}{8}$ Yellow	$\frac{21}{42}$ Blue	$\frac{75}{150}$ Blue	$\frac{31}{62}$ Blue	$\frac{11}{22}$ Blue	$\frac{7}{14}$ Blue
$\frac{50}{100}$ Blue	$\frac{9}{36}$ Yellow	$\frac{11}{44}$ Yellow	$\frac{32}{64}$ Blue	$\frac{30}{60}$ Blue	$\frac{6}{12}$ Blue	$\frac{60}{120}$ Blue
$\frac{4}{8}$ Blue	$\frac{7}{28}$ Yellow	$\frac{16}{64}$ Yellow	$\frac{3}{12}$ Yellow	$\frac{8}{16}$ Blue	$\frac{40}{80}$ Blue	$\frac{12}{16}$ Blue
$\frac{9}{18}$ Blue	$\frac{25}{100}$ Yellow	$\frac{6}{24}$ Yellow	$\frac{8}{32}$ Yellow	$\frac{19}{76}$ Yellow	$\frac{48}{64}$ Blue	$\frac{5}{10}$ Blue
$\frac{10}{20}$ Blue	$\frac{17}{68}$ Yellow	$\frac{12}{48}$ Yellow	$\frac{13}{52}$ Yellow	$\frac{20}{80}$ Yellow	$\frac{25}{100}$ Yellow	$\frac{14}{28}$ Blue
$\frac{35}{70}$ Blue	$\frac{8}{32}$ Yellow	$\frac{10}{40}$ Yellow	$\frac{15}{60}$ Yellow	$\frac{40}{160}$ Yellow	$\frac{14}{56}$ Yellow	$\frac{5}{20}$ Yellow
$\frac{21}{28}$ Blue	$\frac{12}{24}$ Yellow	$\frac{40}{80}$ Blue	$\frac{15}{30}$ Blue	$\frac{33}{66}$ Blue	$\frac{15}{20}$ Blue	$\frac{75}{100}$ Blue
$\frac{2}{6}$ Green / $\frac{5}{10}$ Blue	$\frac{12}{36}$ Green	$\frac{9}{27}$ Green	$\frac{30}{90}$ Green	$\frac{20}{60}$ Green	$\frac{11}{33}$ Green	$\frac{6}{18}$ Green / $\frac{2}{4}$ Blue
$\frac{18}{24}$ Blue	$\frac{5}{15}$ Green / $\frac{9}{12}$ Blue	$\frac{15}{45}$ Blue	$\frac{8}{24}$ Green	$\frac{10}{30}$ Green	$\frac{3}{9}$ Green / $\frac{6}{8}$ Blue	$\frac{30}{40}$ Blue

Page 25

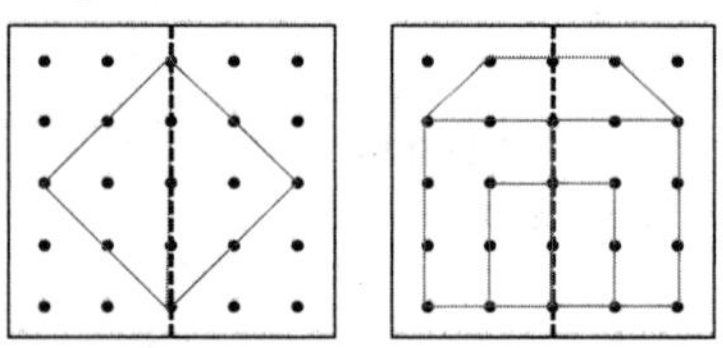

Page 26

1. A, B, D, F; **2.** F

Page 27

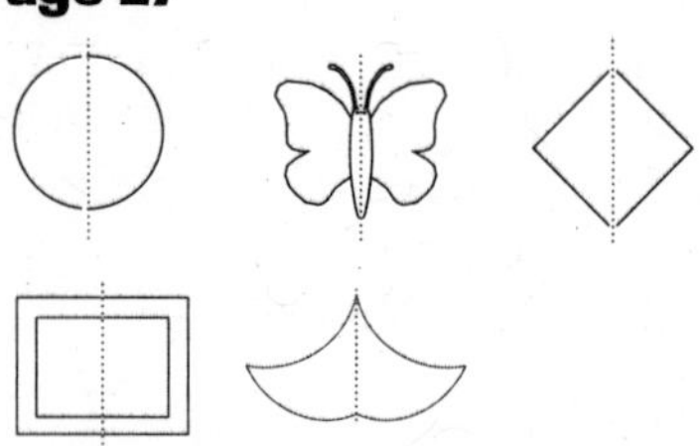

Page 28

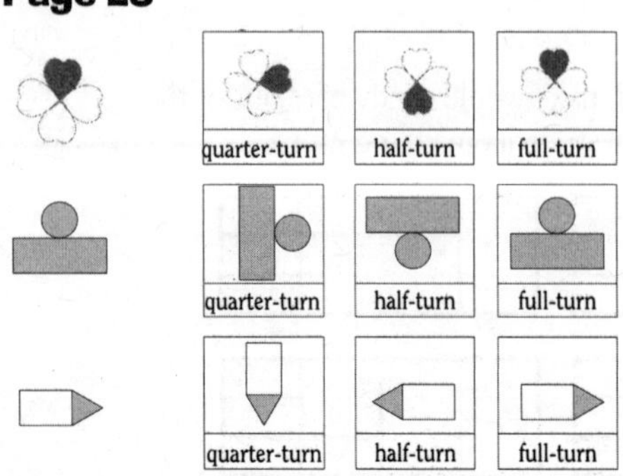

Page 29

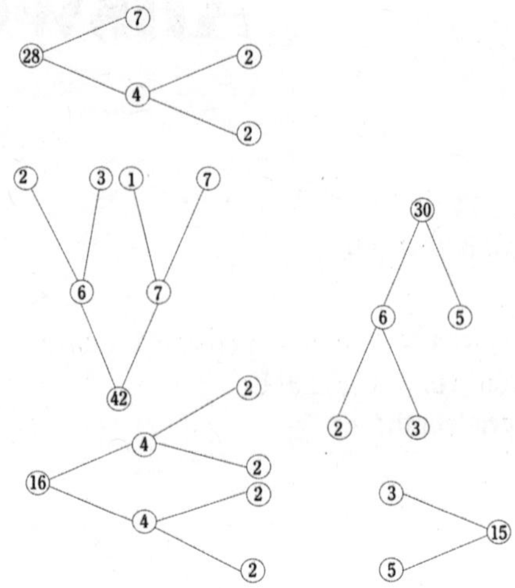

Page 30

IT'S "TULIPS" !

Page 31

1. 27 or 45 or 63; 2. 60; 3. 54 or 72;
4. 333; 5. 125; 6. 2222

Page 32

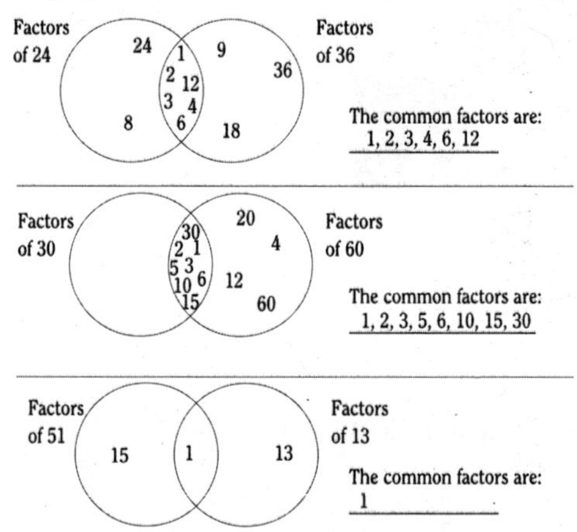

Page 33

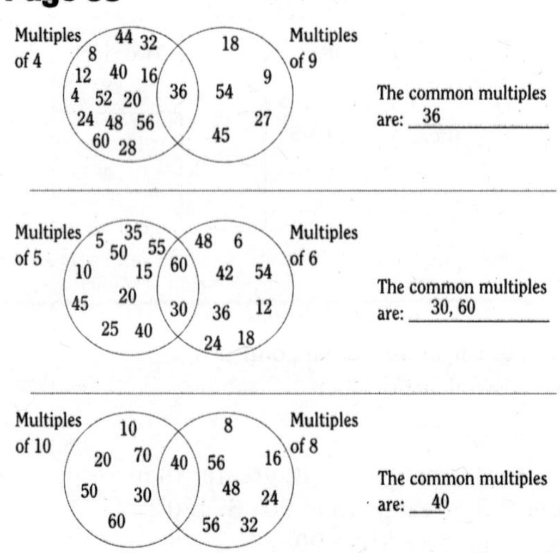

Page 34

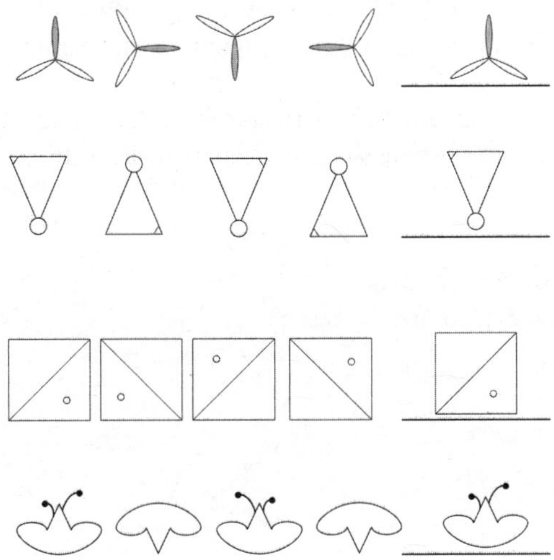

Page 35

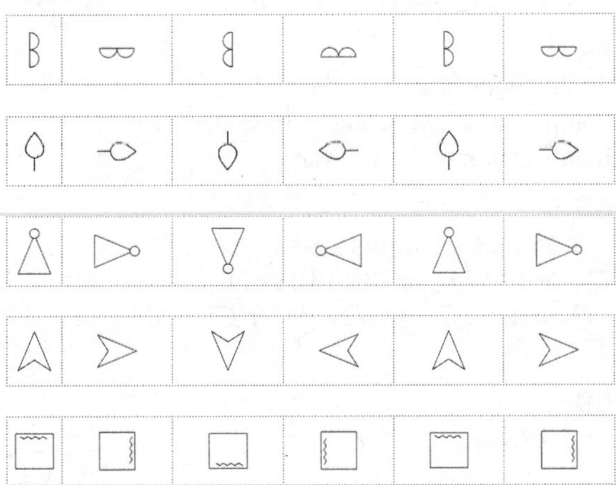

Page 36

24 + 4 + 7 = 35 = 7 + 4 + 24

9 + 11 + 6 = 26 = 11 + 9 + 6

1000 + 7000 + 2000 = 10,000 = 2000 + 1000 + 7000

69 × 2 = 138 = 2 × 69

11 × 10 × 3 = 330 = 10 × 3 × 11

4 × 8 + 1 = 33 = 1 + 4 × 8

Page 37

A.

1	2	3
11	12	13
21	22	23

B.

78	79	80
88	89	90
98	99	100

C.

58	59	60
68	69	70
78	79	80

D.

23	24	25
33	34	35
43	44	45

E.

42	43	44
52	53	54
62	63	64

F.

66	67	68
76	77	78
86	87	88

Page 38

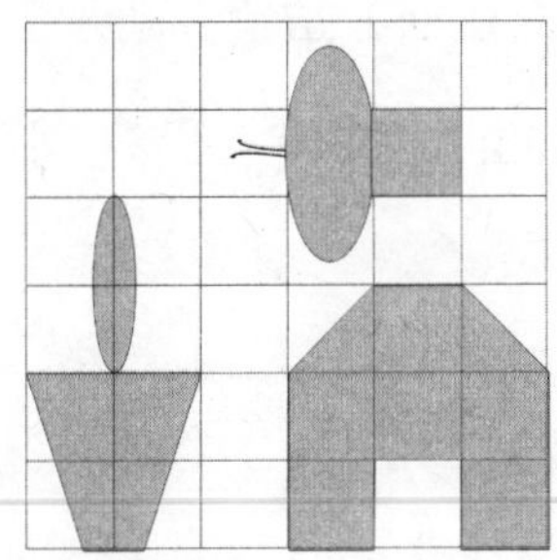

Page 39

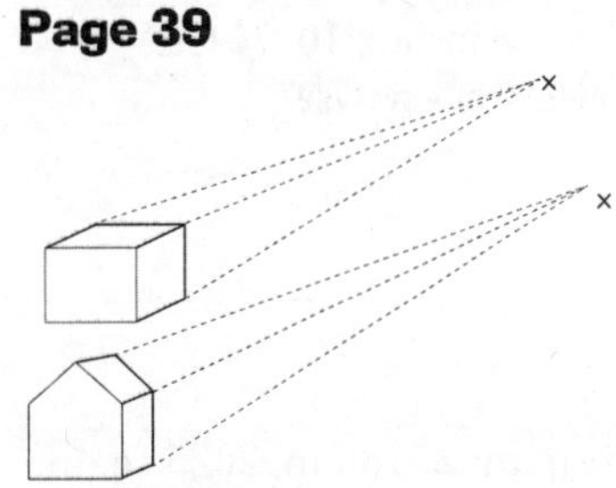

Page 40-41

1. right; **2.** 90°; **3.** Nat St.; **4.** Mat St.; **5.** Hat St.; **6.** Nat St.; **7.** 8

Page 42

1. Judy landed in square A.
2. Down 2 squares and 4 squares to the right. Four squares to the right and down 2 squares.
3. One square to the right and 6 squares down. Six squares down and 1 square to the right.
4. Seven squares up and 5 squares to the left. Five squares to the left and 7 squares up.
5. Answers will vary. Each path does not have to have the same number of squares.
6. He is 1 square down from square D

Page 43

1. 2, A; **2.** 4, A; **3.** 8, E; **4.** 9, D; **5.** 4, B

Page 44

1. B; **2.** D; **3.** A; **4.** C

Page 45

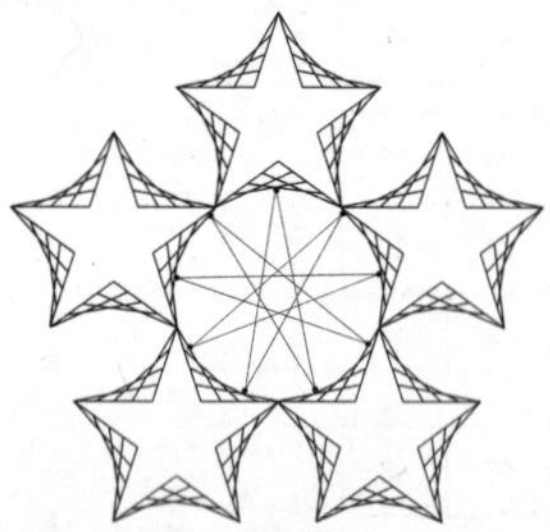

Taking It Further: 0.70 = 0.7; 9.007 < 9.70, 0.30 = 0.3; 6.900 = 6.9; 0.90 > 0.09

Page 46

ACROSS: A. 3.7; **C.** 4.38; **E.** .55; **F.** .6; **G.** .9; **J.** .57
K. 7.16; **L.** 4.3
DOWN: A. 3.14; **B.** 76.29; **C.** 4.5; **D.** 8.1; **F.** .2704
H. 24.3; **I.** 1.7; **J.** .36

Page 47

1. ₹1.55; **2.** 23p; **3.** ₹2.45; **4.** 48p; **5.** ₹12.70
6. ₹3.51; **7.** 32p; **8.** ₹10.65; **9.** 83p; **10.** ₹2.57

Page 48

1. 16; **2.** 20; **3.** 19; **4.** 40 inches; **5.** 12 inches
6. 9 inches; **7.** 55 inches; **8.** 30; **9.** 38 inches; **10.** 74 feet
Why do people with colds get plenty of exercise?
Their noses run.

Page 49

Answers will vary.

Page 50

1. 90 m; 45 m; 270 m; 4050 sq. m; **2.** 180 m; 2025 sq. m.
3. 410 m; 9750 sq. m.
Super Challenge: Answers will vary. Check to make sure students have not answered by dividing the perimeter in Q1 by 2.

Page 51

1. Add four crackers (units).

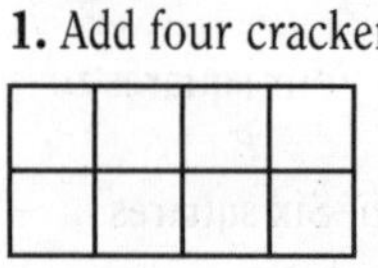

2. The area will be 9.

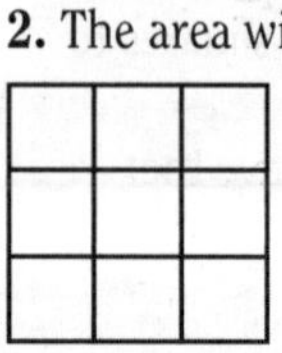

3.

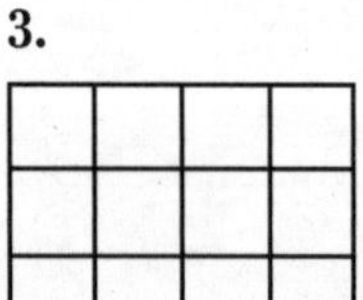

4. Possible answers include: a square 4 units by 4 units with a perimeter of 16; a rectangle 2 units by 8 units with a perimeter of 20; a rectangle 1 unit by 16 units with a perimeter of 34.
5. Answers will vary, but any correct answer will use 24 units.
Super Challenge: One possible shape is a square made of 16 units.

Page 52

1. January and December; **2.** 35°
3. June, July, and September; **4.** Yes; 5°
5. No
6. Warmer
7. Fall
8. May
9. 20 degrees

Page 53

1. 30 dB; **2.** 30 dB; **3.** 20 dB; **4.** 20 dB
5. 40 dB; **6.** Jet Plane take-off; **7.** 120 dB

Page 54

1. 15 kids; **2.** 3 hours a day
3. Less than 1 hour a day; **4.** 6 or more hours a day
5. Less than 1/2; **6.** Answers will vary.

Page 55

1. 4 x 71; **2.** 78 x 43 + 1; **3.** 143 x 8 – 7
4. 18 x 734; **or** 18 x 743; **or** 73 x 184; **or** 74 x 183
5. 418 ÷ 71; **or** 418 ÷ 73; **or** 471 ÷ 83; **or** 473 ÷ 81
6. 83 ÷ 17

Page 56

IT CUT A CORNER

Page 57

1. 11,000; **2.** 24,000; **3.** 30,000; **4.** 56,000; **5.** 1,00,000
6. 1,44,000; **7.** 2,10,000; **8.** 2,56,000; **9.** 3,60,000; **10.** 3,75,000
Why did the spider join the baseball team?
To catch "flies"

Page 58

1. 4;
2. 20 remainder 10
3. 11;
4. 6 remainder 58
5. 9 remainder 7;
6. 9 remainder 50
7. 5;
8. 33 remainder 12
9. 30 remainder 40;
10. 40 remainder 30
A Comb

Page 59

1. 4000; **2.** 3750; **3.** 625; **4.** 1500

Page 60

Answers will vary.